ONE NATION INSIDE THE BRICKS

GANGS, VIOLENCE, AND VICTORIES!

by

Jake Manning

edited by Colleen Skerry Giannino

ISBN-10: 1500494968
ISBN-13: 978-1500494964

In this book, I have recreated events, locales and conversations as accurately as possible from my memories of them. Some names and identifying details have been changed to protect the privacy of individuals.

More info:
www.onenationinsidethebricks.com

Book Design: Y42K Publishing Services
www.y42k.com/bookproduction.html

Photography:
www.christophersargentphotography.com

Table of Contents

Dedication...5

Foreword..7

Introduction...11

Chapter 1: My Beginning......................................15

Chapter 2: Case Studies 30

Chapter 3: Gangs: Then and Now 51

Chapter 4: The Streetworker 55

Chapter 5: Vigils and Memorials........................65

Chapter 6: Cemetery..69

Chapter 7: Street Corner 73

Chapter 8: School 77

Chapter 9: Family...81

Chapter 10: Public Transportation 85

Chapter 11: Sports Locations..............................89

Chapter 12: Street Cred 93

Chapter 13: Life in the Field 97

Chapter 14: Solutions 131

Glossary of Terms...141

Dedication

This book is dedicated to my Mother, who did the best she could with what she had. Single moms, especially in The Bricks, know how hard it is to raise a family by yourself.

She raised 5 boys and a girl, or as she used to say, five Kings and a Queen!

Margaret Manning-Quigley

My family: Kevin, Marty, Paul, Bill, and Eileen.

Special thanks to:
- Mr. Cornelius "Connie" Linehan
- Mr. Jack Kennedy
- Mr. Frank Sullivan
- Mr. Gerald P. Casey
- Dr. Stephanie Hartwell
- Mr. Matthew Fiorenza

For all the single parents and grandparents working hard to raise a family in The Bricks.

For all those who work with people on the streets.

And to all the kids waiting around the ice cream truck…

Jake Manning

Foreword

About three years ago when I was working with a Boston-based non-profit, evaluating their programs addressing gun violence, I attended a community forum. At the forum, I began fishing around, casting my net, trying to identify the local players on the front lines. First responders are an interesting group, and I wanted to know how they did their jobs, survived the vicarious trauma of confronting trauma, and if they believed they made a difference. I did learn that many individuals are not in these jobs for long. I was told to understand why I ought to spend some time shadowing front-line first responders. So my next question became "who?" There do seem to be many folks in this community who have great ideas, some who even seem to thrive on the adrenaline of the work fueled by guns and fear, but I was less inclined to speak with those individuals for any length of time nor shadow them. One name came up repeatedly though. "You need to meet Jake Manning." "I know who you should talk to, you should talk to Jake." "Jake Manning and his Streetworkers."

That afternoon I met Jake. He was a blend of equal parts thoughtful, spiritual, and respectful. It was apparent he was good at what he does, but he did not glamorize the work in anyway. Similarly, he was curious if his work and that of his team, the Streetworkers was effective. We made a plan to keep talking - to stay in-touch as we both wanted to know more. I could help him evaluate the program and he could help me understand this community based work managing trauma and gun violence. I also spent an afternoon with him on the job.

The Streetworker program is run by the City of Boston's Center for Youth and Families. The Streetworker team, Jake included, all managed to take their own life experiences and turn them around to try to improve their communities. Jake's book is a case study in entirety about overcoming the odds, rising above or being brave enough dissipate violent currents in the city including gang life, and understanding the delicate and tactical approach to do so. In this context, he elucidates the roles of social institutions including family, schools and transportation in the context of this violence and the trauma to communities that are so familiar with memorials and vigils that there are norms in the way they are conducted. He understands his team, a group of largely younger and minority individuals who have not been privileged in life. The team understands the financial, territory, and cultural currents that underscore street life. While Jake does suggest that something in the street has changed, he writes of a "fundamental difference," "the lack of respect for human life," a sociologist such as myself might put it differently. This book illustrates some of the fundamental causes of the breakdown of social mores. For individuals living at or near street life anomie prevails where brute force and gun violence perpetuate the cycle of violence and normlessness. This is what Jake is writing about. What comes through, however, is against this backdrop there are still good people that chose to turn it around; to try to make things better; to contribute to the solution rather the problem. The trick is to get to a point where there are more of them, more Jakes, than guys with guns.

Stephanie W. Hartwell, PhD
UMass Boston
June 19, 2014

Jake Manning

Introduction

I lived in public housing for over 20 years and worked there for many more after that. I grew up in Boston, in the Old Harbor Village (McCormack) housing development- just a few blocks from where the notorious Whitey Bulger lived. This is a pseudo-reference about the area and time that I lived in the bricks near him. This was a different time for sure.

When I started working as an Area Youth Worker for the City of Boston's Youth Activities Commission, I was assigned to a geographic area based on police districts and had a case load of about 20 young people. It was a different time back then but with some variation the concept remains intact. The challenge and the position have changed over the years as the dynamics of working with inner city youth has changed.

Today, most Outreach Workers will say that they work with young people who no one else wants to work with. They engage on the street corners, playgrounds, and basketball courts of the City. They speak with young people at bus stops, outside schools and many other public venues. They advocate and support young people in court and schools. The Outreach Worker will attend family meetings with government agencies, such as the Department of Youth Services, to discuss the options and future of a young person. Many times the Worker on the block knows the young person best because he or she comes from a similar background. This common ground helps to build a relationship of trust. Trust is the cornerstone of engaging a troubled young person in a dialogue about making healthy choices and thinking forward about getting on the right path.

It is helpful if the Outreach Worker comes from the same background as the person in need of guidance. If they know the Worker has been where they are it carries impact and hopefully influence. The path is tough but the venue is vital to connecting these young people who most often are not connected to anything. It can be quite a process that takes time and a person with a lot of hope and a lot of patience. Sometimes when the usual resources have been tried it takes an Outreach Worker to make the connections.

This book is about the people who fight the daily battle to live in decency and with dignity. Although I had little in the way of material things, I had family and extended family. This is about some of the things that bound us: music, food, drugs, alcohol, poverty, and wonder. These things cross all defining lines of ethnicity and religion. They work together to remind us all that at the end of the day, we are all "One Nation Inside the Bricks."

Chapter 1: My Beginning

I woke up dazed, confused, disoriented and covered in blood. After I anxiously checked myself for wounds, my first feeling was an egotistical satisfaction and relief that none of the blood was mine. It must have been quite an event, I think. This scenario was typical of events in my life at that time. The present (and the future if there was one) was unknown, uncertain and volatile. The way I was going, my life seemed to be leading in one of three directions: jail, an institution, or an early grave.

Hope was not even existent in my life at that time. It was a time of certain uncertainty, explosive violence, and rampant poverty (financial and otherwise). Feelings of hopelessness brought on an approach to things that spoke of recklessness and non-direction. If I wanted something I had to take it. I had nothing so I had nothing to lose.

If I saw someone wearing a nice watch and I wanted it, I took it. Hopefully it wouldn't involve a struggle. Someone could get hurt that way. The train station was the best place to find victims. A victim could be someone who looked at me the wrong way or perhaps someone from out of town. These are the ones I would prey on. If the victims were in a group I would always go after the biggest guy first, usually the rest would scatter. I was taught to always go after the biggest kid because the rest of the group would think I was crazy and I was.

Add a few drinks and my liquid courage kicked in. I could be taller, stronger, and faster, so I thought. The world was mine. It certainly wasn't anyone else's, if I was in it. I was nurtured in a world of violence, so I became just that. I learned what I lived and I lived what I learned. I couldn't keep my eyes on the prize because I'd never seen it.

As a kid I witnessed the ravages of alcoholism and all the dysfunction it brought with it. As a kid coming home from school I didn't know if I would be hugged, kissed, or slapped. The fear of the bottle was everywhere. It lied within the unkempt home, the dishes in the sink and the empty bottles strewn about. How can I be raised with any stability when all I knew was the opposite? Even on good days it was still the wonder of what would it be like when I got home from school. It was a long walk especially with no gloves, holes in my shoes and insufficient clothing to guard against the winter's cold. The saving grace was that there was always cleanliness, or attempts at it. My mother, a single parent, had to work overtime as it was, to keep my brothers and sister clean. So, that was a good thing. Poverty was never an excuse for being dirty. We could always afford soap, for the most part.

Yes, we were a family but it's not what you think. We had tough dynamics going on. There was not a lot of room for tears, excuses, or I love you's. It was more about survival. It was about survival in the bricks. I lived in a housing project. It was a six family brick building with about twenty five kids living in it in all. Many of our neighbors were in a similar situation – trying to stay afloat with limited resources and no knowledge of where to get more resources. Yes, the rent was cheap but the cockroaches and mice weren't paying their share. I didn't dare leave any food out because it would be gone.

It's amazing that somehow I survived. It was about eighteen years of welfare peanut butter and those five pound boxes of cheese. I ate peanut butter and jelly almost every day. Some days I had the luxury of a grilled cheese. I was grateful to have food because sometimes I had bread sandwiches and some days there was nothing. This was the reality in my world. What could I do at eight years old and there was no food? I had no options, so I waited. I waited and wondered if and when some food would show up. It could be a long time. This was a challenge to the spirit of a young person, or old for that matter.

I would stand by the project window, slightly opened, and gaze in wonder. I wondered if there was anything out there for me. There had to be something more than this. Life couldn't be like this for everyone – an everyday fight for a chance to find some hope. Some hope for a better life. It all seemed so distant. I couldn't keep my eyes on the prize because I'd never seen it...this phrase reappeared in my life many times.

Summer nights in the projects were always a challenge. The melting heat permeated the bricks making it an oven-like experience. Of course, we couldn't afford air conditioning and neither could most of our neighbors. Distant and temporary relief could be found in the ice cream truck which made its daily and nightly runs through the area. The caveat was that I didn't have any money for ice cream or much else. There was always some brief comfort in seeing the truck pull up though. There was some hope that maybe I would have a small financial windfall or that a bystander or neighbor would kick in for me. There was always a feeling of helplessness as a kid when I sat and watched others have a cooling ice cream and I couldn't even afford that. It's sort of rock bottom for a kid to work it in his mind that it was ok. It was ok not to have what most took for granted. The thrill of the ice cream truck soon passed as my hopes melted into the night. A sweaty and uncomfortable night dressed in heat and uncertainty.

As a kid, summer mornings during baseball season were something to look forward to because my little league team had practice and the coach always brought a cooler full of soda. It amazes me to this day that it was such a big deal. My coach was a great family man and I'm sure it was not easy for him to give his time to us and take time away from his own family. He was always very kind to kids on the team. He always encouraged us and rarely, if ever criticized. I believe he realized that many of us did not have a dad at home and he knew he was a role model for us. God bless him and people like him.

There was some semblance of stability in being on a team. It was a place to belong, a place that I was part of something. It also represented some form of discipline and commitment as there were practices to attend and games to be played. There was jealousy in the fact that other kids would have a dad, uncle or some family member attend a game or two throughout the season. That was beyond a dream for me. My family life was sporadic and tentative at best. My mother was probably more likely thinking of ways to secure some form of dinner for us than attending a game. I have grown to realize the vital importance of simply showing up. It was not necessary to scream and shout support at a sporting event or the like. It would have been enough for my eyes to simply see someone there for me. As a kid, once again, I rationalized and justified all the absences through all the years.

On mornings when I had to get up for school I didn't know if it was a saving grace or a dread that existed in my thoughts. School could be an emotional safe haven. As I would trudge along with holes in the bottoms of my shoes, I felt my feet get wet as the rain made its way into my socks and shoes. Inside I knew that things shouldn't be this way but I also knew that people do the best with what they have. There may be kids somewhere who have no shoes at all. I would always tuck baseball cards in the bottom of my shoes to keep the water out, but it was a futile effort. There were long winters back then and trips to and from school seemed like quite a trek. Gloves or mittens were not common instruments against the cold. The good part was that I was certainly awake when I got there and was glad to embrace the heavy heat of a classroom.

I always did well in school because I didn't want to bear the wrath of my mother! I saw what happened to my brother when he would not reach acceptable goals, and it wasn't pleasant. My brother was and is gifted with God given intelligence and developed common sense. Back then, it was all about school grades and support although nurturing comments were hard to find. In retrospect, I know that you can't give away what you don't have. It's no secret that parenting is the hardest job in the world yet has the least qualifications. Try doing it alone and you really have a challenge in front of you.

After my parents divorced, I moved into the Old Harbor Village housing project in South Boston. Today it is called the Mary Ellen McCormack Housing Development. As a seven year old my father would come and pick me up on Sundays to take my brother, sister and I out for the day. Unfortunately, he would bring us to various barrooms in Dorchester or we would wait in the car and play as he went in for a few drinks. It wasn't bad for a while but if he was gone for a long time, it was painful, especially on a hot day. We would play games as best we could, look out the window and wonder about the world going by.

At such a young age, I didn't know that I didn't know; that this was unacceptable and unhealthy for the spirit of a young person. Sometimes we would get to go into certain bars and play pinball and eat chips while having a soda. We liked this as we were the centers of attention and strangers would give us money to play the various games in the bar or to buy candy. Our dad did his best with what he had. He was always very kind and pretty quiet, but he enjoyed his beers too. It's a tough thing how alcohol can grab a hold of someone and taint their sense of right and wrong and what's good and not-so-good for themselves and others around them. I never felt any sense of wrong doing by him. My gut told me that he was just having a few beers while enjoying us as well. I know better today. Once in a while he wouldn't show up to take us. I don't know if I was happy or sad about this. We all loved to ride in the car since we didn't have one of our own.

In the summer my family and I would go to the South Shore to visit my cousins in Marshfield. We all loved it there. You might as well have told me I was in Hawaii because the feeling was that awesome. My aunts both were born in South Boston but married and moved to Marshfield. It's a great seaside town and the water was always very clean and very cold. It was great to be paroled from the projects for a few days. As one could imagine, it was a whole different world to us - a world of nice homes with backyards and treehouses. Wow! I could relax there. After all, they had cookouts and lawn games! As comforting as it was, the project kid inside me was always vigilante and ready. I learned to cope and survive. I did so without even realizing it. I became a scrapper, internally and out.

I remember seeing a dog corner a squirrel one day. The squirrel lunged and bit the dog in the forehead and killed him. You did not want to corner me either. Many times I would think, please don't mistake kindness for weakness. You will pay a price if you make that mistake. Survival of the fittest indeed!

In life, sometimes people get paid off, to look, or not look a certain way. I remember my first payoff. I was four years old. My mother had gone out and had a few beers and then had a car accident. The family was gathered in our home. I remember looking up at all the adults. Some engaged in spirited discussion, others passive but all were concerned. I felt like a plant gazing at giant Sequoia trees I knew something was going on up there and I knew it wasn't good. Finally, someone acknowledged my presence before I was stepped on or knocked out of the way. Then it came, a package of Hostess cupcakes. It's like stack of 100's to a four year old. I took it and found my way into the other room. No one said anything or tried to explain anything. The proof was in the payoff. I wonder how that impacted me in a lot of ways. To this day, I cut to the chase and don't have a lot of time for lengthy explanations or dissertations upon the simplest of things. Some people may say I am impatient as I nurture their intent to get to the point. So, a system of sorts was established that day. I just can't remember if they threw in a glass of milk with my cupcakes, for good measure.

Summers were always long and hot in the housing project. I simply didn't have access to the resources that others may have had. I had no air conditioners, no car, and no direction. The heat and the environment were stifling. Some days were spent going to public pools like Charles Street. I would also venture into the Boston Common's Frog Pond. I loved it there as a kid. It was like Vegas to me and my brothers and sister. We could play there all day and take time for a peanut butter and jelly sandwich or two. It was a great experience as getting out of the project for the day was not very common. The whole train ride and people experience was a healthy adventure. Sometimes living in public housing made me feel like I was mentally trapped. I was reluctant to go outside of where I lived. There was a sad comfort about staying where I felt safest, even though I hadn't really been anywhere else. I knew who I was and where I was, when I was in my own neighborhood. I felt vulnerable outside, but I would never show it. That would be a sign of weakness and that was not acceptable.

Sometimes when coming from the Charles Street Pool, we would get robbed. Kids from other areas of the city would take our money and on occasion, our sneakers. We would only have fifty cents or so, just enough to get home on the train. I remember going to the train station and telling the Transit worker, and he would always let us on the train for free. I am so glad he did because we were kids and had no idea how to get home from there, other than taking the train. I have no resentment against the thieves. It's all about survival and that's something I understand. I just wish they hadn't taken my sneakers, unless they were their size?

When I was about nine or ten, I couldn't sleep. I was awake and restless. It was a hot summer night with an open window affording me no comfort from breeze or fresh air. I heard some voices outside and sat up to look out the window. I saw several men getting out of and approaching the trunk of their car. They opened it and pulled a large sort of sack out of there. It looked like one of those large military bags you see soldiers carrying sometimes. I thought nothing of it and finally fell back to sleep. In the morning there were a lot of people and police around and focused in the area where I saw the men and the bag. I told my mother what I saw and was immediately told that I saw nothing.

There was a dead woman in the bag and for some reason, they decided to drop it right there in the middle island of a main road. I lived on the edge of a main artery in and out of the city. When things like this happen, you are told to stay away from the windows and not talk to anyone about what you saw or didn't see. It's just the way it was. I could have unknowingly endangered my family, even at nine years old, by sharing what my eyes saw. It's a push back when I was trying to do the "right thing". It sure helps confuse a young person and makes a person question their ethics, but only to a certain point. I somehow understood that parents know something I didn't and I had to trust in their knowledge. I would back my feelings and thoughts out, and then go and watch cartoons. 'Nuff said or not!

When I was in my mid-teens and my brother, a Marine, was in Vietnam. One day a knock came at our door. I answered and there were two Marines, one with flowers in hand. As my mother approached the door from behind me, one of the men asked, "Do you have a son in the Marine Corps?" She said, "Yes" and both of our hearts fell to the floor. It was a surreal moment. The exchange seemed to happen in slow motion but it ultimately took years of life out of me. One Marine asked, "Is his name…?" My mother said, "No. His family lives down the street but his aunt lives one floor up." They had the wrong house. It was a mistake that should never be made again. It was sad enough that we knew the guy without adding this additional trauma to it. A very sad day as we learned our friend and neighbor had been killed in action in Vietnam.

I really believe it takes a bit of life out of you when you experience something like this. I certainly will never forget this incident. My sadness and heart go out to the Marines who had to deliver this message as well. They quickly realized their mistake and were composed but clearly understood the devastation. In short, they had been at a residence a couple of buildings away from where the deceased lived. When no one was home there, they were told his aunt lived up the block. So, they were seeking her residence in hope that the deceased's mom might be there, but she lived one floor up. We told them to go upstairs but never knew what happened after that. My thoughts and prayers will always go out to the family. I will never forget that day or the ultimate sacrifice made by neighbor.

As I got older, I started making poor decisions and using alcohol. It's amazing to look back and realize how much my drinking impacted my life. I simply didn't know that I didn't know. After I barely escaped high school, I was lost and had jobs here and there. Some friends had moved to Florida and were working basic jobs down there so I decided that might be a good idea. I saved enough money to get a plane ticket and headed off to Tampa. The really bad part is that I didn't tell my family. Once again, I made another poor and selfish decision - one that I would pay the price for.

When I arrived in Tampa, I gave the van driver the address and went on my way from the airport. After driving around the neighborhood a bit the driver said this address did not exist. Of course I had no phone number or anyone to contact down there. I guess I was a typical disorganized teenager?

I panicked and decided to call home collect. My brother answered and said my mom didn't want to talk to me. I could not blame her. I had gone off the path again and didn't deserve to have her speak to me. I didn't tell her or even say goodbye when I left. It was such a shameful and bad decision that I needed to own at the time.

So, I had about twenty dollars in my pocket and figured I better go to a bus station and see how far north I could get. I made it to Raleigh, North Carolina. That's where I started to "thumb." After walking more than a few miles and failing at my attempt to hitch hike, I lost hope and gave up. I stopped thumbing but kept walking. I got mad at God and told Him off. I questioned why He had brought me to this point only to leave me abandoned. The walking went on for quite a while then out of nowhere, a car pulled up and asked if I wanted a ride. I was startled but happy to get a lift and quickly replied, "Yes!" The driver brought me to a fast food place and bought me something to eat. This was good because I hadn't eaten in two days, except for a candy bar. I continued on my way with a full stomach and some hope.

As I continued along route 95 North I saw an eighteen wheeler pulled over about a half mile up. I ran toward it as I assumed it had stopped for me. As I stepped up to reach for the door handle, on the side of the door, it read, *Casey and Hayes Movers* South Boston, Mass. I was absolutely shocked and in disbelief. I opened the door and the driver was adjusting a pair of headphones. He was surprised to see me as he apparently had not stopped for me. I asked, "Are you going to South Boston?" He answered, "Yes!" I said, "I am too". He was as surprised as I was but said, "hop in!" I couldn't believe it. It chills me to this day. This was one of the very few times in my life when I had lost all faith. It really was quite a lesson. In my heart, I went from hell to Heaven. I had failed the test of my faith. Even though I gave up on Him, He did not give up on me. Thank God for God!

In my late teens I volunteered at a teen center in the projects where I lived. The center was in one of the basements of a three story, six family building. It was a great space and a safe place to chill, play some board games, lift some weights, or just get out of the cold. It kept kids off the block and out of the hallways. As part of my commitment there, I would walk the area and let young people know about the center. It was my goal to have people come in and check the place out. For the most part, everyone knew each other so word spread quickly as it always did, in the projects.

One night, right before Christmas, I was heading out to the local store and some younger kids stopped me and said there was a party nearby and no parents were home. I went up to the apartment and young kids were running around and acting up. Someone had written in magic marker on the wall. The apartment was a mess with things all out of place. There was no sign of the Holiday - no tree, presents, or decorations. I quickly found out that their mom left and said she'd be back in a few days. It was a blessing that I knew the kids in attendance at this apartment. They realized this was not going to continue. I had everyone pick up a bit and leave the house. These girls who lived at the apartment were about nine and eleven years old. Their guests were older, which could have made things much worse than they were when I arrived. I had no choice but to call the police.

This scenario was and is totally unacceptable. How could

a parent leave young girls to fend for themselves with little food and no supervision? This is one of the first events that triggered my passion to help people who are less fortunate or simply in need of support. I could not stand by and do nothing about these types of situations. I often wonder what happened to this family. After they moved out of public housing, I was not privy to their new location or circumstances. The sure thing is that many other situations came forward after that, with different families and different scenarios. My passion was nurtured by the challenge.

After a couple of years as a volunteer, I found a job as an Outreach Worker for the City of Boston. My domain included the area I lived and worked in. This was perfect for me. I had already invested a lot in my community so it was nice to get a paycheck for my efforts as well. They told me I was the youngest worker they ever hired. They were taking a chance on me. I was proud and grateful for the opportunity.

In addition to a geographic area, I was assigned a caseload from the courts and schools and other local referral sources. At nineteen years old, I received my first case. It was really off the hook. There were so many tough pieces to it that it almost had me quit.

The young man I was assigned to work with had attempted suicide. His home life included an incestuous relationship between his father and sister. His parents were well-educated so there was no obvious appearance of concern. Once I got involved and developed a relationship of trust with this young man, he opened up and dropped a lot of heavy stuff on me. Although I would always work to maintain professional standards, I couldn't help but sit at home at night and thought of ways to have the perpetrator taken care of. After all, I was still a street kid and I still had local connections to people who enjoyed putting child molesters, in their place. I would have at least a few drinks and fantasize about the demise of such monsters. They should be terminated with extreme prejudice. Thank God I never acted on my feelings about this case. I eventually turned it over to folks with the proper academic as well as law enforcement credentials.

If that was my first formal client, what could the future hold for me? Did I have the spiritual fortitude to deal with things the right way? Would the street kid in me overtake my emotions and cause me to make poor decisions? I guess I had to focus on the good part of that scenario, that a kid who had tried to take his own life found enough trust and enough hope in me to share very personal information about himself and his family. I had to hold on to that understanding and realize that lives can be saved even if the spirit has a long climb out of despair back to a path of re-born trust.

Jake Manning

Chapter 2: Case Studies

My story is not unique. It is a sad truth but generations of families are born into this type of life. Some people, me included, find a way out. In short, I became the person I needed. People somehow wind up on the right path and are able to rise above the negativity. Others cannot and eventually succumb to the ways of the street. Along my journey I have met people with some amazing stories. Here are three of the more memorable:

Jasmine

Jasmine's story is one of incredible challenges against the odds. She's twenty-four now. She grew up in the projects with her mom and one little brother. He early years were filled with uncertainty and much despair. Even as a little girl she knew things weren't right. She witnessed a lot of dysfunction and violence in her home. How can a young person feel safe when there is so much chaos? A family built on drugs and alcohol and relationships toward those two is very unhealthy. There is no real family structure here. Life is all about take what you can get when you can get it. Food is not a priority. A cold slice of pizza sitting on the kitchen table in the morning is gold. Even at eight years old, she knows about survival of the fittest. In case you're wondering, there is no microwave to heat it up. It's a miracle there's a toaster. So, that's how it goes.

Every day can certainly be an adventure but it's never a good one. There is no safe place in this house. There are no emotional safe havens either. Her family is an intoxicated mess. They have their own stuff and hardly acknowledge the presence of a young girl in the house. Yes, she gets a bag of chips or a sub here and there or sometimes it's just a mayonnaise sandwich. At this age, you don't know that you don't know. In most homes this would be unacceptable, but not here. It's the norm; it's the way it is.

Sometimes Jasmine walks up to the playground to get out of the house. It's not good there but it's better than sitting home and listening to people yelling and watching everyone getting high. There are strange men there sometimes and the way they look at her makes her uncomfortable. She doesn't know how to express her concern about this and wonders if anyone would listen or do anything about it anyway. At the playground, older kids smoke weed and seem to be there for a similar reason. Most don't seem to have a worry. Maybe they're high and don't care? Cars keep pulling up and they go to the care for an apparent exchange of money and drugs. She doesn't get too close as she hopes they will pay her no mind. The one broken swing is enough to entertain her for a while. The slide is dirty but that's ok. A few minutes of relief from home is always welcome even if she gets a little dirty. A few other kids show up at the playground. They have a similar look about them as they make the best of this space as they can. It's like everyone knows what's going on but no one wants to talk about it or simply can't put into words what's going on. The younger kids all avoid the older kids and do what they can to entertain themselves. It really is a small world, especially when you feel like you're in it by yourself.

As night falls, there is a dread in returning to the house.

Of course, she has to go home sometime. Jasmine wonders if anyone misses her or even knows she's gone. It's a feeling to get used to. A young person needs and wants to be acknowledged. We all want to be part of something right? Is it too much to ask to be acknowledged in your family? When the dog is out for too long they ask about him. She wonders where she fits in. She wonders about self-worth and self-esteem. These areas are impacted for the rest of her life. Jasmine is on a path with no direction and no positive energy. How can she go forward in a place where no one cares? We learn what we live and we live what we learn.

As she gets older and starts to experiment with substances, she feels the temporary relief others feel from the use and abuse of alcohol and other drugs. She embraces the temporary euphoria that is readily available in her family home. Her mom enjoys seeing her getting high as it offers a warped sense of mother/daughter bonding that she hasn't known. This is the start of something new and beautiful? They can finally chill out together and have a true mom/daughter relationship thing going on?

Jasmine is in her early teens and she finds all these men stopping by a bit uncomfortable. They look at her with eyes that don't tell her she's safe and it's all good. She definitely doesn't want to be alone with any of these creeps. She tries to share her concern with her mom but her mom quickly pushes aside the conversation. Her mom says they are her friends and she should relax and enjoy herself. Jasmine finds no comfort in this. As time goes on, she reluctantly joins everyone in the kitchen as they get high almost every day. She still keeps a guarded eye on mom's various male friends. She knows they could be trouble.

She starts to miss school more often these days. She's sleeping late and watching TV a lot. She really is following the path her mom seems to have taken. No one speaks of this, it's just there. She just keeps it movin'. No one tells her about options or life choices. No one tells her that she can be a doctor, lawyer, a cop or a nurse. There is no prize to keep her eyes on.

As Jasmine awakes one morning, she staggers out of bed to answer the front door. In her dazed state, she doesn't look through the peephole and just opens the door. It's one of mom's drug dealing friends. She tells him her mom isn't home but he convinces her to let him in for a minute and he will get her high. People know how this goes? After getting smoked up a bit, this dude starts making advances on her. She pushes back but he gets even stronger and more insistent, like he wants her to fight back. A few muffled calls for help go unanswered. She is raped on her own couch in her own living room. This dude threatens to kill her mom if she says anything. What's left of her spirit is devastated. Her emotions are all over the place as she searches to find a way out of this mess. He leaves the apartment like it was a friendly visit. She struggles not to grab a kitchen knife and stab him. That may not be a good idea. This has to be one of the loneliest places in the world; left with devastated feelings and the violation of her body and spirit.

Should she call the police? No, they will turn it all around as they know what goes on in here. Call a friend? There's no one she's close enough to share this with. Tell her mom? Well, she has to tell someone! It seems like days before her mother gets home, although it's later that afternoon. Her mother is upset because this guy called her and said that Jasmine had come onto him and he had sex with her. He made up a bunch of BS to add drama to his story and turned it all around. Mom is worried she could lose her drug connection. Her priorities are blurred by her addiction. This is so unacceptable but it's reality. This violent animal has turned this house upside down. Jasmine's mom refuses to believe her and scolds her as she beats her for doing such a thing. Jasmine has jeopardized one of her mom's drug connections, a lifeline for an addict. She is warned not to tell anyone lest she get a real beating. She is a young woman trapped in a world of pain with no foreseeable way out.

As life deteriorates, the state dept. of social services gets involved. They find out about the home life and know that this is an unhealthy environment for a child. They quickly remove Jasmine and her brother to a foster home. Jasmine's grandmother fights for custody but it seems she would be just too much for her grandmother to handle at her age. So, off to a temporary foster home they each go. Her brother is not with her. As she tries to settle in to her new space, it's clear that, although this could be good, it's a very different space.

Moving from the projects to living with a white family in the suburbs is quite the move. It takes time and patience to adjust, and she has neither really. She becomes antagonistic and a bit aggressive. The fact that there seems to be a lot of alcoholic the new home doesn't help either. The father is an aggressive punk. The state sends her to counseling as it's required as a support service. The counselor seems stuck on when she was potty trained. He gives her the creeps. She can't deal with this dude. As things continue to slide at the new home, the head of the household gets aggressive there as well. His family is all out and he comes home with a few drinks in him. His wife has the boys at a hockey game and there is no one home except Jasmine and him. He was being all nice to her when he suddenly grabs her by the back of the hair and slams her on to a day bed. Her body goes into shock and terror mode as she is attacked once again. After the sexual assault, she lay lifeless and numb. His threats are hardly audible as she struggles to regain herself. She labors to her feet and barely makes it to the room. How can this happen? She thought these were supposed to be good folk who cared about others' and offered their home for sanctuary?

She lay in bed for two days as the mother of the house assumed she was just sick. The mother brought her some cereal, etc. a few times but her appetite was not there. She is so sickened in her stomach and soul. She is locked in to the fact that no one will believe her if she decides to share what happened? That smug and violent thug rolls around the house like father of the year. Her spirit has received another life sentence, with no parole.

Jasmine is in her early twenties now. Life has not become easier by any means. She did a few stints in state prison for various acts of violence. It hardened her even more to get into the "joint" and learn how the system works. No, not their system, the system the inmates have. She learns quickly to defend yourself and her interests. She knows you have to watch your back and not blink, even for a second, as it could make the difference between life and death.

She is back in the 'hood now, back on the block. It seems she is always an emotional wreck. She smokes a lot of weed and can get it easily. She is in a relationship with another woman and really digs it. She can be really good and fun to be with most of the time. She says that we have our struggles and we do get high so that in itself can lead to problems. She has always sought a place to belong, to fit in. She never had a safe place to just be herself and feel at least ok with it. She simply had no sense of family or any stable place to exist.

This is where her "set" or gang comes in. These dudes that she rolls with are pretty cool. Many of them are here for the same or similar reasons. In this gang she has recognition and she has power, personal power. No one here screws with her. Yes, she carries a "burner". She actually has a few of them. It depends on where she's rolling and what's going on. That's how she decides what to pack.

She was out clubbing one night and a dude kept bothering her. She told him once to step off and he laughed it off, but left. Later on he came back after probably having a few more drinks. She gave him one last warning, and then blasted him in the leg. He caught a .40 slug in his thigh and was bleeding like a pig as she quickly walked away. There was a big crowd in the club and it happened so fast that no one knew what went down. The blaring music was replaced by sirens as police and ambulance pulled up outside. She passed the *burner* to another gang member and he left quickly even before her. She had to get rid of the piece quickly as the law was on the way.

She got out of there and was never caught. She hopes that bitch learned his lesson. Sometimes people think that just because you're a woman you can get over. It isn't going to happen like that in her world. She will not be a victim anymore, especially when it comes to men. She really hates men. They screwed her over and took advantage of her almost all her life. That party's over.

In the gang she runs with, she leads the pack. She orders the *work* to be put in. If someone screws with someone in her world, they will pay the price. The price depends on the severity of the offense. She will make the judgment and have the sentence carried out. Almost all of her gang members are guys. That's right! She runs these guys. They respect each other and they know she isn't playin'. If they want to run with her, there will be work to put in and they will be expected to carry out her orders. She has access to weapons and weed, two things they all seek. They carry a guarded respect around her as they know she will do what she says, no matter what the level of violence at hand. They know her reputation and they know she's for real. They also know that once you're in with her, you're not getting out. If you know the workings of a *set*, we cannot jeopardize that with someone stepping out of our gang. You know too much. So, forget leaving the set unless you plan on being missing or deceased. That's how it works.

Dashawn

Dashawn is twenty three now and it's a miracle he's made

it this far. I met him when he was sixteen and living in the projects with his mom, two sisters, and his grandma. His grandma was a typical grandma who was filled with love and concern for her family and yet struggled to meet the challenges of the same, with regard to her daughter and her lifestyle. Her daughter didn't have a lot of money and the money she did have, she used to get high. She would barely provide the basics of food, clothing, and a splash of love.

Dashawn grew up hard and tough. There's simply no other way unless you want to be punked your whole life. He had one or two fights a week growing up and that's just the way it was. His sense of survival was developed by the situations that he was confronted with as he went through his life. He found a way to get through it and to keep it moving.

He and his sisters grew up watching their mom get high and associate with some strange folks over the years. Some people were cool and some weren't. As a kid he did't have a lot of say in things so he did his best to just get by and keep to himself. Dashawn's relationship with his sisters was strained from day one. They just never got along. It's so difficult when there's so much tension and dysfunction in a home on a daily basis. He was a young man growing up with no positive male role models and living with four females. I simply can't imagine any good impact here when you add substance abuse into the mix.

So as Dashawn grew, so did his sense of rebellion. He started chillin' with the wrong crew at school and then after school as well. He found some power in the group. He had some say in things and enjoyed that role. In simple terms, we all want to be acknowledged somewhere. Hopefully, it's at home and as part of our family. If not, we will seek acknowledgement somewhere else.

As Dashawn's role and relationships grew in the group, he began to get into trouble for robbing people and fighting. He did a few short stints in the Department of Youth Services. I don't believe he learned much while incarcerated. I think it hardened him even more. He enjoyed creating fear among his peers. He would extort money from a few young guys as well. He walked a paved path of negativity and violence. This was his place where he felt power and a sick sense of comfort. Some young people enjoy, to some degree, being locked up. They get three meals a day, cable TV, and basically hang out all day.

As life went on, he became more involved in things. He got swallowed up in the rush and fallacious power of gang activity. He dug the notoriety and the fear that preceded him. He developed a false sense of security on all levels. His ego stepped in and told him he was all set that he had nothing to worry about. The reality is that he had a lot to worry about. There were people out there looking for him. It's amazing the way these guys fool themselves into thinking they can roll through any neighborhood whenever they feel like it. There are many dead who thought the same thing. Once again, the ego and the power can lead you on to one last ride.

When Dashawn was twenty years old he was shot four times in broad daylight. He was in close proximity to a hospital so he received medical attention in a fairly quick time. It happened with a lot of people around so at least one person dialed 911 and got a quick response for an ambulance. They say it's what saved his life. One bullet went through his side, two others were removed at hospital, and the other one could not be taken out as it was in delicate spot and removal could kill him. So, he has lived with that for a bit now. He also has a colostomy bag which is very uncomfortable at times and is certainly a burden, but at least he's alive. He cannot play sports, etc. like he used to.

People around him knew something like this was coming but there simply wasn't a lot they could do about it. Dudes may not want to post up with you if they know you're about to catch one from the other gang or friends' of theirs'. No one will verbalize it, but that's the way it is.

When Dashawn was at home recovering from this incident, he found out he had a baby coming. His girlfriend is filled with mixed emotions. She knows someone just tried to kill him and now her future is looking tough. If they get a place together, how will that go down? Will his enemies seek him out in their home? These days there are no rules among gang members so the answer is yes. Opposing gang members have shot at grandmothers and over the heads of children if they know they live in the same house as someone they are looking for. There have been some very close calls and some direct hits as far as this goes.

The decision is made for her to stay with her parents and Dashawn stays in the bricks. He has to be careful to sneak around for a visit with his woman and child as he doesn't want anyone to know where she lives. This is a dangerous trip to visit your own child but a safe and delicate ride has to take place.

The logistics of operating in the gang world are tough. If a person wants to survive they can never be too careful. Sometimes dudes get smoked up or get to drinking and make a poor decision. That's the one their enemies are counting on.

Dashawn finds out his sister is having a child. She is having a baby with a guy that's involved in a gang that rolls across the other side of town. It's not a rival gang but with something like this, it's not good. Dashawn puts word on the street to find out who this punk is and what kind of street cred he has. Although he still doesn't get along with his sister, she's still blood. His grandmother is really feeling the strain and pain of all this drama especially because of its attachment to violence. In a quieter family setting this may or may not be welcome news, but it's just not that way here. The poor woman struggles to maintain some sense of positive attitude with her family as her daughter continues to be out of reality and still getting high, watching game shows and drama all day, and being out of touch. It's a shame but that's the way it's going down for now.

I can't help but wonder who would want this kind of life. In talking with folks on the block they say it is what it is. What's that mean? I had my challenges growing up but for the most part, we were always safe and didn't seek to compromise that by actively seeking activity that would threaten that safety. We need to continue to help young people find their passion and develop some sort of plan to assist them in getting there.

Time goes on and Dashawn has moved on to find a better

sense of life and things around him. He and his girl are living in a town just south of the city. He still struggles as his past is a serious deterrent to finding a viable career. When you go on a job hunt and your criminal record comes up, an employer is understandably reluctant to put you to work in their business. He sells a bit of herb on the side and his girl has public assistance as they hold up in their section 8 subsidized crib. Dashawn still has medical issues related to his being shot a while back. He is semi-focused on the well-being of his son and his girl. It's a tough spot when you can't shake free of the past. It will be a long process for him but at least he's taking some responsibility for his son and his future. It's tough to protect yourself from people finding out where you live, work, or play when they are intent on paying you back for past occurrences. Dashawn holds on to hope...hope that the light at the end of the tunnel isn't an on-coming train. Deuces!

Yesena

Nine years ago, twelve year old Yesena came to Boston from Columbia. Her life has been a challenge, one far beyond normal for a young woman. She came here with her mom. They were both filled with dreams of a new start with wonderful opportunities. Their dreams are those of many who come here seeking a better life. They believe in the endless chances to improve themselves and their quality of life. They live in an area where about half the people are bilingual, speaking Spanish and English. This was a good move because it helped Yesena to feel comfortable as she learned her way around. Yesena knew some English and started with the

English immersion program offered by the schools. She learned quickly and moved along in class as well as making some new friends and learning about the neighborhood and the city. It was fun and exciting.

One night a friend invited her to party. She was reluctant to go but it was a nice warm night in late spring and school was getting out. So, she decided to go. She had some fun and met a few new people. After a while someone lit up a joint and offered her a hit. She had tried a wine cooler and liked it, so she felt it was cool. This was the start of a lengthy list of troubles for Yesena.

Eventually, she ended up with a boy, Eric, she didn't know very well and had trouble maintaining her safety. He became aggressive when they were alone. She felt terrible the next day, yet somehow, it was all new and exciting. As this relationship grew, Eric asked her to sell some weed for him in school. He gave her some weed and bought her some nice clothes in exchange for her help. She kind of liked getting high so why not get it for free? This was working ok for her. She started to expand her base of friends and became a bit popular in school. She wondered where Eric got his weed. He seemed like he could get it anytime with no problem at all. She eventually learned that Eric was in a gang.

His gang was originally based in El Salvador so she had heard some things about it even as a child back home. Red flags and alarms went off in her spirit. Inside she knew this couldn't be good. Eric had shown her something she didn't have before. He offered her a compromised form of safety. He told her, "You'll be fine as long as you stay with me and do what I tell you." That's the gist of it. We see it all too often in human service scenarios - predator types preying on the unprotected, vulnerable, and weak.

One day Yesena decided to call it quits. Eric said he would meet her at one of the gang member's homes where they usually went to get smoked up.

After getting high and making sure Yesena's guard was down, she was told that nothing was going to change and that she would do exactly as she was told. She was then sexually assaulted by several gang members as well as Eric. She was told that she will be killed if she told anyone or tried to get away. And if she did get away her mother would be killed. Her heart and her dreams are trampled on. She was numb with fear, shame, and hopelessness. Her journey has left her onto a path of destruction. It seems like it's been Eric's plan all along to just use her as he and the gang's need fit.

Yesena staggered through life for the next year, barely making it through school and the daily challenges of Life. It was at this time that she met a Streetworker. The Streetworker met Yesena at a bus stop in the busy center of the 'hood. This is one of the areas where Streetworkers is employed by the City to actively engage young people as they come from school or travel to other parts of the city. The job description of a Streetworker is a complicated one. Generally speaking, they are trained to helped young people find ways to rise above gang life.

A Streetworker will have several conversations with someone to establish a friendship and trust, and to ensure a young person that they are for real. They also carry ID showing that they work for the city. A good Streetworker will also have some common people with whom to reference to a potential recipient of services. That's what happened here as Yesena knew one of the boys that he helped and started to open up a bit.

As time went on and more information was shared, the Streetworker became aware that this was a very bad situation and started to seek street resources to help get her out of this lifestyle she was trapped in. He did not even think of breaking her confidence as he knows the gang culture and knows it could be fatal if they thought she was talking to anyone about her problem.

Over a period of time, this particular Streetworker was able to help a couple of young guys who were involved in gangs. If someone said they wanted to change and asked a Streetworker to go to court and support their efforts, its' something the worker usually would do, if he believed the gang member was being truthful. So, that's what he did. Some things work out and some don't. The end result is that the worker has to establish a relationship where he needed to have one, no matter what the outcome.

Now it is time, to get the favor returned. The Streetworker mentions in a casual setting about Yesena. He asks two of the guys if they know her. They laugh and say they do know her. It's a delicate conversation as he says he knows her mother and would like to help her get her life together. He lets it go after a brief discussion, only to be brought up a week or so later. Once again, it really is a delicate conversation. It's one that they have to be willing to engage in or as it's a waste of time. They really respect this guy and they decide that she's a waste and she really gets high these days, so they say ok. She can be freed from the gang connection she has. They say the bitch is useless anyway and they have a couple of new girls working things.

The Streetworker is ecstatic but can't show how pleased he is. He had told them that his mother and Yesena's mother knew each other back in Columbia and he thinks that part of the conversation hit home for these clowns. Whatever works, right?

That week, they gradually back off of her. Now, the real work begins. Now, the task is to get her on the right track. What is she passionate about? What does she you want to do with her life? What makes her tick? Yesena makes slow but gradual improvements in her life. She doesn't smoke weed as much because she can't get it as easily as before. She doesn't want to go back to where she used to get it. That's for sure. She makes slow improvements in her relationship with her mother. The thing is that she's moving in the right direction and the Streetworker makes sure she knows she has support and encourages her to do the right thing and encourages her to start making some goals and plans as to where she wants to be in the future. He also introduces her to some healthy young women who are living right and making healthy decisions for themselves.

Yesena makes it out of high school, but not by much. Her grades were not good, but it's a done deal now. As she is frightened by the future, the Streetworker sets up a meeting with an admissions counselor at a community college. This is a person with whom he has an established connection.

After the meeting and eventual admissions process, Yesena is accepted at a community college, where she is still in attendance as of this writing. She pretty much keeps to herself and her studies and has a part time job three nights a week.

Her journey is far from over. The emotional challenges of the past haunt her on occasion, as expected. The Streetworker had suggested that she get in contact with a social worker so she will have someone to share with in an objective setting. He also found a support group for female victims of violence that is offered by a local hospital. It took her about six months to go to that and she has said that she doesn't share much but listens a lot, and it's been a big help just to listen. So, the group is there for her to share if and when the feeling comes across her to do so. I am just glad she's going.

Jake Manning

Chapter 3: Gangs: Then and Now

Although it is possible to identify common themes between my story and these case studies it is important to highlight a fundamental difference about the times. In younger days, gangbangers agreed upon an unspoken set of rules when it came to enacting violence. Today it seems to me that the only rule is that there are no rules. Gangbangers that were around in the old days knew that there were parameters around violence. An attack in a public setting where innocent people were would never occur. An attack on a guy with child or innocent folks just wouldn't happen. Believe it or not, there was an unwritten code about gang violence. There was a hint of respect that all would adhere to. If not, you would be dealt with. From what I have seen with today's gangs, there is total lack of regard for human life. These guys don't consider by-standers or children. They have tunnel-vision and just focus on the hit they want to make.

There was an incident in which a father, who knew he was being sought out by a gang, brought his child to the playground. It was a nice sunny day and kids were out everywhere. Everything seemed to be all good until a dude on a mini-bike came slowly up the street the wrong way, pulled a gun out and started firing into the playground. He had apparently seen this guy, followed him, and the rest we know. Fortunately, neither was hit nor was anyone else. Word on the street was that his family gave him a beating for taking his child to the playground and putting her into danger like that. Maybe he was thinking they would never pursue him if he was with his daughter? This was not a good calculated risk.

Perhaps, drugs or alcohol had clouded his thinking.

Another time two rival groups unintentionally met in a local pizza place. Violence erupted and three people were killed, with one bystander shot as well. Who knows what impact this has on a person or family who was there and had just stopped in for a slice of pizza? There are certainly many psychological effects. Obviously, personal safety is at the forefront. If you had been there would you ever go back? What about any pizza shop you go into in the future? The point is that the trauma is there. It's in your heart and your spirit. Others may recover from physical wounds but psychological wounds are very different.

There was situation a few years back where a child was accidently murdered during an incident of gun violence. As word spread throughout the streets, people found out who did the shooting. After a bit of time went by, that person disappeared. Some say he moved down South and others knew better. The only sure thing on the street was that he would not be seen again. The law enforcement community may or may not know who did it. At that point, it didn't matter. It was taken care of, although the short life of a child was gone. Hopefully, the message was clear: there are boundaries and if you cross them a price will be paid. This kind of unspoken code is from the old way of the gangs and doesn't exist today.

One Nation Inside the Bricks

Jake Manning

Chapter 4: The Streetworker

Streetworkers deal with a broad range of feelings as they tend to their clientele. You can have a young person in front of you one minute and then shot and killed the next day. How does a person address that? There is no doubt that my Streetworkers experience prevalent feelings of helplessness and hopelessness that seem unrelenting to the spirit. Many Streetworkers themselves come from challenging backgrounds and have fought the good fight and the not-so-good fight. Some have been gangbangers. The sure thing is that no one has lived a privileged life. Any piece of mind or success has come at a price. Some of my workers have physical wounds from shootings and others have emotional wounds from various parts of life. The key is they turn it around use their experience to help someone else. That's what makes it worthwhile. There's straight up good and a splash of restitution in it all. Who would have a problem with that? A person can find themselves in a win/win situation that way.

This is where a Streetworker can be invaluable. Typically Streetworkers are from the community and can offer an opportunity to share with someone who's sort of "been there" in terms of being familiar with the situation. Many Streetworkers have been involved in making the wrong decisions in their younger years. They use their experience to help others now and there's nothing more valuable than experience, especially in this venue. They go into places that others dare not go into. I mean this in a geographical as well as emotional sense. It's sensitive and tender territory and you have to know the lay of the land. It really makes for a most effective approach to a delicate situation. If a worker doesn't know a family, he knows someone who does know them and they validate his "street credentials" and most likely will open an inroad to assisting a family in need. No, it's not always perfect, but it's the best approach and we usually end up helping in one way or another.

Many times when someone's hurt in gang violence we can find out the parties involved and work or prevent any further violence. Ideally, the greatest victories lie in the fact that we prevent a violent incident before it happens. This happens more than one would think, but it's an intangible and therefore hard to document. It's a very delicate and dangerous process to deal with gangs and gang members. Do I have to say it's a volatile group? After a staff member works his way into a group and identifies the leaders, it's imperative that he has their trust. The tactful approach to a group rests on many factors. Caution is paramount when approaching a group that is using marijuana or alcohol or other drugs. Behavior may become unpredictable and if gang members are carrying "heaters" staff will probably keep it moving. It's just not sensible to try to have a conversation with someone who's high - save it for another day. It's best to check in for a minute with them, keep the conversation light and then step off. One of the keys is to let the community know that the door is always open. It is important that people know who the Streetworker is and what they represent. The Streetworker exemplifies a different way of life and living - a life away from constant violence but filled with clear conscience and hope.

Streetworkers try to pass on the message that it is possible to live in a place where there is peace and a family can be raised where they don't have to see what you've seen. It is necessary to find out what makes the person in need tick, what they're passionate about and then how would you get them on that path. It's a challenging and lengthy process sometimes.

The streets are unforgiving, relentless, and insistent. The codes of misanthropic remedies are hard to fathom. For example, a young man was shot because he gave the wrong answer when asked where he was from. A group of young men down the street had been asked the same question and said nothing. As a result, people on the streets wanted the first group to retaliate because they did not answer when asked by the assailing group, who went down the street and killed someone. How can this be logical at all? They want someone to respond and they figure these younger guys are not schooled enough to tell them where to step off. Why aren't the alleged leaders doing something about this, if anybody? I mean they caught the shooter who did it. Can't you let the law take care of it? Simply answered, "no". The streets have their own rules no matter who gets caught or doesn't get caught. Street credibility may be on the line. If they get away with it this time, they'll be back and do it again, if they feel like it. Gang members want to make sure rival gangs know they will have to pay a price if they return and look to put "some work in." The message is clear: no one will enter "our" block without paying a price.

Many gang issues are financial, some are territorial and some are cultural. The Cape Verdean community is an intricate web of family and friends and sometimes enemies. Some of the violence can emanate from the fact that there are several islands in Cape Verde and on occasion an incident can come from the various factions that live on any given island against another island. There have been occasional cases where a distant relative has actually shot someone in their own family who lives or has lived on a different island in Cape Verde. I realize this is very unusual but it's true. The blinders of violence can muddle many a person's eyesight. Sometimes people get so angry or caught up in a situation that they simply act first and ask questions later. This adds to the obvious sadness of a violent incident when you learn it was someone connected to you. It is an incredible challenge when you have violence take place right within your family and people start to draw loyalty lines depending on what information they have or have access to. This further diminishes the ability of a family to recover in any way when it's as close to home as it gets. Even time cannot heal this type of wound.

In my opinion, prayer will always help if people are open to such, which is not the norm. People are already mad and blame God for their loss, so why would he help the now. There can be a devastating seed of discontent and misanthropy that surrounds a person's spirit and simply takes over. I have seen people settle in to a place where they hate or strongly dislike everyone. It seems their life is ruined and they take no comfort in seeing others who may have some happiness or contentment. It's a mountain of emotion that may not be climbed in this lifetime.

If the leaders of the family have fallen to this degree, it is with guarded optimism and hope that I can work with and help a sibling of someone who's been shot and or even murdered. A child will see his parents in agony and adopt that stance. Sometimes there is a sense that young person is betraying his parents if he doesn't get in line with their emotions. They feel they must support their parents by staying where they are emotionally or face the possibility that they are emotional traitors. How can you move on when someone shot your family member? The feeling instead is centered on exacting revenge – this is seen as the duty of the surviving family member. These are all real considerations that a person goes through. I can't imagine the range of feelings that one has to deal with when they are confronted with a violent situation. Prayer, counseling, support groups and a person who can impact a family's emotions in a positive way are all welcome strategies to help a person move on in a positive way.

The Streetworker is the connection. He may be the only person who can contact and connect someone to resources that they may not have otherwise found. The venue of connecting with people on street corners, at bus stops, and outside of schools, can be crucial to helping someone find the help they need.

Streetworkers have to meet people where they're at on many different levels, and that sometimes includes geographically. Workers never know where they will have an opportunity to engage with someone and impact their chosen path...or just widen it.

The proximity to violence can rest upon a fine line

between a person's past and their present. The impact and influence of a Streetworker is highly dependent upon one's experience in the streets and how he brings that to the position. Folks will tell you the streets are unforgiving. If you did some "dirt" years ago and have cleaned your life up, it doesn't mean you get a pass for the future. There are still those who want to deal with you, "to get even" or settle a score, in their mind. A Streetworker is always on guard against the past as well as the present.

Streetworkers need to have a keen sense of their environment and be fully conscious of their surroundings. There is no time for daydreaming when they are in any given neighborhood. They can be at a community event, a transit stop, or a family event - It simply doesn't matter. People intent on violence do not take breaks or have downtime. Some carry weapons in hope of coming across someone they've been looking for. There are no passes. Living on a path of violence means always being armed; it's just part of the lifestyle choice. There's a good chance alternatives have been offered but simply haven't been taken advantage of. Or the person has chosen to pursue something different. There's a sad acceptance about this among some young people. They seem to view it as a valid option in life. The thought of living your life looking over your shoulder twenty four hours day offers no appeal to most people. The excitement would wear off quick. A person living the violent lifestyle is very limited in many ways including where they can travel to and what school they may go to, where they might shop for food or clothing.

For example, there was a confrontation in a local pizza place that left three people dead. They all simply went out for a slice of pizza, and never made it home. I just can't imagine this happening in the mainstream of things. In the world of gang members, it's reality.

The relationship of a Streetworker to a gang member is based on trust which is developed over time. There has to be mutual respect and trust if anyone is to get anywhere under these conditions. To me, this is when it's all on the line. This is the ultimate challenge and test. This is where no police or any other group can stop someone who is intent on perpetrating harm on someone else. This is the triumph of street work and I've witnessed it many times. We need to continue to find and build with young men and women who are sick and tired of seeing the violence. Some have lost friends and family and others have been victims as well. They know the field and they know the game. Most importantly, they are capable of developing a trusting relationship with gang involved young people, and sometimes not so young gang involved people.

Streetworkers need to have the balls to walk up to a street corner and *chop it up* with these guys. They need to feel comfortable in this venue. If not, they don't have a chance. The streets will eat you alive and spit you out. If a worker shows any fear, they are done. It's a process to share intentions and speak of resources to gang members. Many times it's good to have someone who knows them, introduce the Streetworker and then go from there. Oftentimes, there is a relative or someone in the community who can do this and validate a worker's position and intentions. Trust has to be earned.

Workers can advocate for someone at court, help them back into school, and maybe connect to a GED prep program. The first contact or two is the key to success or else there will be nothing to build on. I train staff about their approach on several levels. They will pick their approach and always keep in mind that timing is paramount.

One Nation Inside the Bricks

Chapter 5: Vigils and Memorials

Vigils and memorials are a common part of the grieving process in most cases. A vigil is usually held the night after someone has been killed and is usually at or near the site of the crime. On one occasion I arrived at a vigil site before anyone had shown up. I could feel an impending sadness in the air that would soon develop into reality when people, young and not so young started to arrive. Some brought pictures, others held candles but all were dressed in disbelief. The process of understanding and accepting death at a young age is quite a challenge. Many young people think they are invincible and will never die. As pictures and dialogue peeled away the denial, raw emotion came pouring out in a flood of tears. Sometimes young folk are just there and kicking it about this and that and then realize that this is a vigil in remembrance of someone. I suppose that behavior is a part of the slow process towards acknowledgement and eventual acceptance.

Sometimes neighbors in the area of the crime do not want a memorial site in front of their home. It's a delicate situation that may need to be addressed very carefully. When people gather in remembrance, some tend to get liquored up or smoke some weed. This can lead to all kinds of problems. The police will keep a respectful distance, usually a block away, unless people start getting too loud and start disrupting the neighborhood. Some memorial sights have been up for days and there is fear regarding who should take one down and when to do so. The census seems to be that the family of the deceased should be consulted if possible. They can in turn inform peers of the victim so that there is no misunderstand and people are respected. Sometimes a staff person may visit the home where the memorial is and talk to the homeowners. Most are understanding and patient about what's going on.

Many times friends will visit the site where someone was killed on the anniversary of the incident to pay respect to the spot where they were last seen alive. On top of the obvious sadness, opposing gang members are aware of the anniversary as well and may drive by and pop off a few rounds. This is really crazy and has added disrespect, but it does happen and does nothing more than perpetuate violence.

One Nation Inside the Bricks

Jake Manning

Chapter 6: Cemetery

A visit to the cemetery will always raise feelings to the top again. It is only human to revisit the story of each young person when you go back to where they are laid to rest. Some of the graves are unkempt while others are alive with plastic flowers and personal tokens of lives taken much too young. When I visit someone's grave who has lived a reasonably long life, it's different. I have a different sense of "rest in peace". I really have a stronger belief when someone is older. It's just not so for a young person. They have hardly lived and yet they are gone. It sends a parent, sibling, or friend on an endless journey of wonder. A person seeks to make any sense of it. The spirit of life presents a daunting challenge when its path is so short.

As the sun fades, so does the hope of a family that has been stricken with violence. The question is whether or not their faith will rise again on another day. Does the family still have the will and spiritual fortitude to climb above this tragedy and live another day? Do they want to find some sense of recovery? There really is no way to know the answer to these questions. It depends on the type of personality and emotional depth of a person as well as their Faith. It's easy to say that love conquers all, but what if it were you in this situation? As human service workers we walk a very fine line here. Water seeks its own level. I have to be very delicate and understanding as you hope to assist someone to climb out of their pain. It is a tender path indeed.

Each time I visit the cemetery, I hope the deceased know that they are remembered by lots of people, even virtual strangers like me. It's tough to learn about someone after they die. I hear the stories at the wakes and after burial gatherings. "He was a good kid…He always helped his little brother and loved his sister beyond words…He also worshipped his Grandma who practically raised him." These are the types of comments I hear. It's all good to hear but we still have a young person that is no longer with us. It is necessary to examine his other life, his secret life that some knew about and some didn't. There is a prevalent denial sometimes about who a person was and what kind of lifestyle they lived. This is not about offending those who have passed on. It's about having some real conversations about how our young people live and the realities and dangers of making the wrong decisions. It's about responsibility and reality. It's the ability to get inside a kid and find out what's up, in a real way. No lies, no BS.

I got into a straight rap with a parent one day who told me her son would come home with money in his pocket that she knew he made selling drugs. He would buy her a fridge or microwave and the like. He would put a stack of tens in her hand. She told me, "I need that boy to work because I need that money. I don't ask him how he gets it but I have an idea. He tells me not to worry about anything."

I tell her it's a nightmare waiting to happen because when someone sees the kind of money he's making, they will want it too. Guess what? They will take it by either killing him or by bringing some muscle to scare him out. Most times a person won't move because they feel they own the block they work on. So, it will end violently. This woman seems interested in buying what I'm selling - a message of hope that she can get to her son. She can tell him. I know they have a taste of cash now and that's hard to resist when you don't see a lot of options but there is a better way to do it. I share some of the options in terms of job opportunities but it is nearly impossible to compete with the lure of a quick dollar.

She's not feeling me so what else can I say? It is my cue that it is time to step off and leave the door open for further conversation if she chooses. What I'm trying to promote is the idea that there is nothing like an honest dollar earned. It feels good to wake up with a clear conscience and move forward in the day knowing you're doing the best you can for your family and doing so without putting yourself or your family in danger.

Jake Manning

Chapter 7: Street Corner

The street corner is theoretically a place of safety and comfort. Gang members feel protective over that territory because it is their spot, their block, their home. They feel invincible...

No one can touch me here. If they try, they better come equipped with something. I'm going to protect my block with whatever resources I need. I'm reppin' this spot. I may not have any play at home but out here, I've got juice in what's happening. I may not be somebody at home, in school, at the gym, at work, or in the joint, but out here, don't screw with me. I've got back up here. These people are my real family. These guys would die for me. They would die for our block. I get what I need here. I get weed and other drugs. I can get a burner, a whip, a woman. I am somebody when I am here. This is my sanctuary, my fort, my real home.

Well, that is the way it supposed to be. This is the way it works in a gang member's mind. The fact is that it's one big fallacy...

No one here will back me up in a real jam. They may shoot with me, but when it comes down to it if it's me or you, you are gone into the night or wherever. This place really provides no safety at all. We are all simply targets here. We are sitting ducks waiting to be taken out. All the things I get here have no real value to helping me. Drugs? Guns? A stolen car? A woman that has seen too many men? None of these things are going to enhance my future. None of these things will help me build anything toward being anybody. Do my dreams stop here on the block or do I want to go beyond here? Has anyone who posted here over the years made it to any place good? I don't think so.

The street corner is where I grew up but we didn't add in violence or violent activity. It was a place to meet and chill with others and find out what's up, etc. We weren't totally innocent, but we sure didn't stand out there with weapons waiting for someone to "ride on us."

One Nation Inside the Bricks

Jake Manning

Chapter 8: School

There was a time when school was a safe place. When someone is involved in gang activity - reppin' a set, they have to be on guard all the time. In a big school, there could be guys from other gangs and that could be a problem. Gang members have to hope that members of their own set go to the same school so they'll have some backup in case they are confronted. It's unlikely that any "protection" can be brought into school. Some young people bring guns and hide them in the bushes or a spot near the school because they know you can't get through the metal detectors. So, if they are threatened in school there's a weapon outside waiting.

Texting is also a feature that is popularly used in school to spread word of impending violence or to seek support around such. I have seen school groups meet in quick notice when something's going down. I have also seen groups change locations quickly - if they arrive at a destination and see a high level of Streetworkers or Police Officers. Typically what happens is a few kids arrive, check out the scene and then text and head somewhere else for whatever is going down. It's hard to keep ahead of this. Streetworkers can only hope to keep up with it.

The safety factor is a huge challenge in school. There are the bathrooms, the gym, the locker room and so many other spaces where gangs can find the victim alone. When a person is gang involved and going to school, there's an added risk to personal safety. This reality acts as the perfect excuse not to go. A young person will rarely say they don't want to go because they are scared. They will say they are sick, they are tired, they don't feel well. It's another dilemma, a catch-22 trap, for a kid that runs with a "set."

One Nation Inside the Bricks

Jake Manning

Chapter 9: Family

When a young person is involved in gang activity, it impacts the family in a big way. First of all their safety is put in jeopardy. If the gang member participates in a violent act and the rival gang finds out where the person lives, well, now everyone's at risk. Many times someone will fire shots into a house where they are after someone. They don't care who else lives there. It could be a three- family home and others' have no knowledge of what's going on. They could easily be victims of violence. A gang banger's siblings are also target. I've had cases of people shooting at grandparents and even adults with little children. There are simply no rules of engagement, no parameters and no ethics. This is war on the streets. The impact will also influence the development of siblings. Some are swept into the life by older brothers and sometimes sisters. They become targets by default, and are destined to respond in the only way they know how. So, the cycle continues.

If a gang involved person is selling drugs and making some money, he may contribute to the household. So, if he's bringing some money to the table, a parent may look the other way. A parent may feel they don't need or want to know where the money is coming from, just that it's coming. Period. It's all good until bullets fly through the window at two in the morning. The parent might have the rent money but now they've got a bigger problem than that. These are tough choices in tough times. What's the safety of your home worth? There has to be a better way than this. It seems there is a prevalent denial of the impact of violence on one's family and home life when there is gang involvement. Some of the guys

I've talked with didn't think people would find out where they live and hunt them down. They figured it would stay on the block or on the street. It's time for some better decisions and hope for a new day and a new chance for the young person and his brothers and sisters.

Jake Manning

Chapter 10: Public Transportation

Public transportation can be quite the challenge when you have to watch out for the enemy. Gang members always have to be careful where they ride and when they ride. Taking public transportation through enemy territory is most definitely a risk. Many public buses have blacked out or canvass covered windows for just this reason - so no one can see who's on the bus. Sadly, over the years, people have been shot as they were spotted on a bus. People followed them and then shots were fired. No concern for the general public, of course. So, now innocent people have to really wonder who they're sitting beside. Just going home from work or school could easily turn into a dangerous situation. You have to watch your back at all times. There could be someone on the bus carrying a gun. That's just reality is some neighborhoods. It is sad, but true. A lot of buses have cameras on board today. This doesn't seem to stop folks from doing what they intend to do. It does however provide clear evidence when used in prosecution. This may be of little comfort to victims' families.

Public transportation is heavily used by students going to and from school so there is a chance to cross paths with those of opposing gangs. As the school year goes on, people know who comes through their territory and at what time. This can be a recipe for disaster. Even with a large law enforcement presence, violence will still take place. Streetworkers post at T bus stops and stations as schools let out. Over the course of the school year they continue to develop relations of trust with young people. Many times a young person will tell a Streetworker about impending violence. The Streetworker has been able to prevent a violent situation form coming to fruition if he or she knows some of the players involved. This doesn't work every time but it definitely has an impact in reducing the number violent incidents that could take place. It's one of those stats that are hard to document; how many violent incidents were prevented? So, public transportation is another venue of concern if you are in a gang. It seems like there are no safe venues when reppin' a set is how you roll. Maybe it is time for a new way to travel?

One Nation Inside the Bricks

Jake Manning

Chapter 11: Sports Locations

Sadly, when there are sports activities around the city, a person has to find out who's playing and attending before they can decide to go. It's basic safety protocol. There was a citywide basketball tournament where the games were designed around who was beefing with who - so they wouldn't be in the building at the same time. Part of me says we shouldn't do it at all if people don't have enough respect to just show up and play some hoop without bringing their drama on to or into the courts. The bottom line though, is safety. It's hard because the good kids who do want to play get penalized because of a few screw-ups who can't lay their beef aside for a basketball game.

I had to cancel a few events over the years where word came from the street that rivals would be "riding" on the courts to do some harm. It's a chance I can't take so it gets shut down. Sometimes college sports tickets are donated for me to give out. Once again, I have to share information amongst works so two opposing sets aren't in the building at the same time. I end up sending rivals on different nights. The idea is to get young people on to campus and maybe have a spontaneous conversation about going to college and playing some ball there. To some kids it's like going to another country. They seem to feel out of place. I know because I have asked them. So, an honest conversation can lead to some positive thinking about the future. Some young people are intimidated by an academic atmosphere, such as a college campus. There are many resources and opportunities to overcome this but people have to take advantage of them.

There are many people willing to help, but you have to be willing to help yourself as well.

One Nation Inside the Bricks

Jake Manning

Chapter 12: Street Cred

Street credibility is a highly valued thing on the block. Who you are and what you're about usually precedes you in the neighborhood. Without some good street credibility a person might as well sit home and watch cartoons. Some people thrive on the fear emanating from their reputation. If someone is known to keep their word, then a person's perspective on any given issue is to be considered. So, if a gangbanger has good street cred and says he's going to do something, people will know if it's a real concern, or just an idle threat. I've seen scenarios where people get ahead of themselves with this and inaccurate word gets out that someone is looking for someone and it hasn't been true. As a result, an innocent person may get shot. The thing is that once something is put out there, it can't be taken back. It takes a life of its' own. Now, it has be dealt with it as best as it can. This is a very serious and tough problem.

If people think you were going after someone and backed out, you may be perceived as a coward. That's the last thing you need. It may bring an unwelcome opportunity for a confrontation. Also, if someone says something about it, they could end up hurt too. The gang world is as much about power as the real world. It's just a far more violent venue and a place where few mistakes are allowed. If someone finds power in their street cred and their reputation, they will go to extreme measures to protect such, especially if that's all they think they have. It's just another notch on the tree of violence, a tree whose roots need to be replanted.

The streetlights penetrate the crime scene as the rain

pummels the pavement. A night of tragedy and apparent random violence is upon us. People gather in silence and share few words about the incident. A young man making his way to the store was gunned down and his body lay in the crosswalk. He is alive as sirens coming from all directions fill the air. An ambulance and its crew are quick to act to put the young man on board and get him to hospital. An anxious silence shadows the crowd. There is a loss for words as there is no explanation as to why a twelve year old would be shot. I speculate in silence. Maybe it's a beef he had in school? Maybe over a girl? Whatever the reason, it's not good enough to shoot someone. What reason is? People are stunned and the cold rain sends them home with no answers. It's always a challenge to get the story behind this story. Sometimes it's just a case of being in the wrong place at the wrong time. Sometimes it's mistaken identity. The streets will hold people accountable for their actions but there's a reckless approach to "street justice." People seek others for revenge and then just attack or shoot anyone in a particular neighborhood who may not be involved in anything. There is no logic or boundary that they won't disregard. That's an added tragedy to an already screwed up sense of retaliation or revenge.

One Nation Inside the Bricks

Jake Manning

Chapter 13: Life in the Field

The following is a sampling of various incidents and circumstances experienced throughout the years. I could write volumes but each of these will give you a sense of the challenge that is presented on the streets on a daily basis.

My journey really started the day I attended the burial of a young boy who was gunned down on a basketball court. By all accounts, he was such a nice kid with a lot of potential. As I approached the site, I realized that in a sea of black folks, I was the only white face. Just for a flashing second, I was aware of this. I have worked with all kinds of folks over the years so I was not self-conscious at all about such things. I just showed up because I wanted to. I didn't think about who would be there and who wouldn't. My consciousness was really raised by the looks of others. I was swimming in an ocean of glances. Almost all were welcoming faces veiled in sadness.

I felt like I was representing white folks in a way. I was honored and humbled in a strange way that still has me searching for words to adequately describe it. My sense was they thought I was some sort of politician or something. This was a powerful and moving experience in my life. I realized fully that I needed to work very hard not to get back to any more of these burials. I needed to dig in and do the best I could, on a daily basis, to stop the violence that is so prevalent in the City. I must be creative and innovative in finding ways to help.

As I approached the Church door, I could feel the sadness permeate the atmosphere. This death wasn't supposed to happen. An 18 year old boy on his way home from a shift at a fast food restaurant gets gunned down, and gunned down in a big way. There was no attempt to wound here. There were many shots fired. I could hear the whaling as I entered the Church. The Cape Verdean community was devastated by a life taken so young. This young life belonged to a nice guy who was working to make an honest living. Some people speculated that the murder was a case of mistaken identity - he was not the intended target. This speculation was little comfort to his sisters and family who had gathered that cold evening to say goodbye. Death brings a sort of surreal presence. When I looked at the corpse of such a young man, it just didn't seem real and I wished it wasn't. As the cold chilled our sadness, the night rolled on with a wave of grief and anger in the eyes and hearts of those in attendance.

There are no real, viable answers to violence. The fact is you don't have to be involved to be a victim of gang violence. It can happen anywhere and at any time. I have seen it at school bus stops, late night parties, and even at services for the dead. The misanthropes have no rules, no guidelines, and no respect, for the living or the dead. One can't help but wonder if conscience is intrinsic? There are various levels of development in such but is the seed of decency there to be nurtured? Sometimes, it just doesn't seem so. I can only wonder what science can tell us about this.

So, daylight came and funeral services took place. The crowd of friends and families brought grief to its height as they realized that this was the last goodbye. As we approached the burial site, mourners began to wail. The cool sun cast a shadow on all hope. There was a feeling of helplessness and surrender. How can we recover from this spiritual devastation?

One of the most challenging pieces of this work is wondering if I will have an impact on a young person. Sometimes it's clear and sometimes it's not. There is no gauge to measure the impact of one human being on another. If a young person turns their life around and heads in a positive direction that is clearly progress.

...

It was another cold winter night as my workers and I posted up outside of the funeral home. An air of cold sadness permeated the crowd that gathered to trade stories and anger at the death of a close friend. There seemed to be no words to comfort anyone, just hopeful challenges to dissuade those who would seek revenge. It was a daunting task played out in informal ways as people came and went in a whirlwind of smoke and rage. As some people cried out in sorrow, others only watched in grief and helplessness. There was no power to restore the deceased to life. This fact was known but hard to accept. You could almost hear the crowd thinking, "There must be something we can do?" The only tangible answer seemed to be reaching out to support the deceased's family and try to help them through this ultimate emotional challenge.

The casket rested at the foot of the altar and his two year old daughter walked up to it, touched it and held onto the corner of it, not fully realizing the extent of her actions. In it, lay her father, whom she will never get to know. I looked at her and thought about her birthday and Christmas and all the special days in a kids life. How would it all be fixed? Who would step up the plate and try to fill the shoes of her Dad? Although the Mass is spoken in Spanish, I knew what was being said. It was the story of a life shortened way to soon. It was about the tragedy of a fatherless child, a mother at a loss for words, and a community praying for solutions. How can people move on from this? How do you recover from death that was wholly intentional and carried out upon someone you love? How do you find peace when someone you cared deeply about was murdered?

As we gathered around the burial ground, a shouting match erupted between two people. It's over nothing. Someone brushed someone too close and didn't apologize. With raw feelings clearly present, it was a volatile situation. Thank God, someone stepped in to calm things down. Now, let his soul rest in peace as tears and rain misted their way into the grave site. Adios amigo!

. . .

It was another night and another senseless crime. Once again my workers and I gathered on the street corner for the vigil for the victim. It was cold and windy so we were the only ones there. We knew that eventually friends and family of the deceased would come. These street corner vigils are a common tradition. As the sun set, people started to stop by with the usual candles and pictures. Everyone expressed disbelief about what had happened, asking rhetorically, *is he really dead*? As the crowd grew, it turned into a cauldron of anger and hurt. The young people in the crowd yelled toward the police cars who sat a respectable distance from the vigil sight. They screamed things like, "Why are you here?" "You should be over where the murderers are!" The crowd started to boil. People tried to step in to calm the agitated ones by reminding them that that type of behavior will only get them locked up. The police were tolerant but have a point at which they would intercede if no one else did. The crowd did calm down which was a good thing because it stopped any further conflict.

The girlfriend of the deceased showed up, clearly expecting a child. Her presence filled the night with tears and shock. Those who had held their emotions became unleashed at the sight of her pregnant body. She was clearly heartbroken, for herself and her unborn child - who will not know his father. As the cold dug in, people slowly started to disperse. It would certainly be a long night for many.

....

My office received news that a young person had been shot. My Team's first course of action is to get on the phone trying and try to find out who the victim is and what associations he may have. In that case, it was quickly learned that the victim was a kid who was just in the office the day before. He came in because he had been released from custody earlier the same day. Someone wasted no time in seeking out this young man of 17 years and ending his life in a violent way. He was shot at close range which may indicate he knew his killer(s). It tore up staff members who had just talked with this guy.

It ate at my soul as I wondered what else I could have done or said. It's a never ending question. I sat there second guessing myself. The real fact is that I'm not responsible for success or failure, life or death, of any other individual. I can hope and pray to have impact but ultimately, it's not mine to own. That simply belongs to God. Then there's the issue of the streets. The streets are unforgiving. They don't care if a gang member decided to make a change in his life. If a person did things out there, there will be consequences, whether it's today or someday in the future. Just submitting a letter of resignation is not an option. It just doesn't work that way. Accountability will come in this life or beyond.

Then it was time to help the victim's family make preparations for a funeral to bury a seventeen year old young man. A life barely lived, places never seen, dreams never realized or perhaps never even developed. Part of the tragedy lies in the fact that dreams were never really formulated. How can you keep your eyes on the prize if you've never seen it? It's a sad and challenging dilemma to help youth reach inside their soul, and search and develop their own dreams and goals. Some are resigned to defeat so young. So, they join a gang where life is not so valued, there is little of tomorrow, and yesterday is far gone. They live for the day, and sometimes don't make it through the night. As we gather once again near the site of the shooting, neighbors and friends stand in the cold and shake their heads in wonder about a young man who is no longer with us. Rest in peace

....

Sometimes there are no words to describe things like the horror of a mistaken victim. How do people reconcile with God when their loved one has been taken by mistake? He was the wrong kid at the wrong place. The shooters were looking for someone with a distinctive hoodie and he had close to the same one on. A young man coming home from a late night shift at a fast-food restaurant and he gets gunned down. He was doing the right thing. My sense tells me it doesn't get more humbling than that for a young man. I mean, he was trying. No one's getting rich working in such a venue. It just doesn't make sense. Someone once said, "Seek not to know the answers, only to understand the questions." Well, this is going to take a long time, especially for the survivors in this family. They certainly have a long way to go. So, the crowd gathered. Many people came and went out of the wake as leaves blew along the street. Passers-by went about their evening; some with looks of wonder and others just kept it moving along.

The next morning as the funeral began, some who had just heard the news showed up with faces of disbelief and sorrow. The emotions ran very high. The feelings of helplessness and powerlessness pervade the crowd. Some gathered silently in a corner and seem to whisper of revenge and payback. The service was sweet and sorrowful. The pastor tried to find some words of comfort. It seemed by the looks on the faces in the crowd his words did not hit home. As we headed off to the burial ground, the finality of this process seemed to penetrate some people. Sudden bursts of anguish and rage came from the young who have gathered. The grave site is a final resting place for some but not for all. Many were reluctant to leave the area. It was a last chance to hold on to someone who had already passed on. There was a sense that not leaving would somehow maintain the life of the deceased. Balloons and doves were cast into the sky in a final ceremonial action. As people looked up to the sky, the sun slipped out of the clouds but just for a minute and then back. That's the way it went down on that day. A day filled with sorrow and endless questions about another life ended much too soon.

.....

Word came into the office that there was shooting in broad daylight. The shooter got out of the car, got into a shooting position and fired about six shots into a car containing two men. There were witnesses but the operative word is *were*. When the police arrived everyone had amnesia or didn't have any idea what happened. That speaks to the code of the streets. Usually this silence means "We know who did this and we'll take care of it ourselves." People whispered in the crowd as the ambulance pulled away. Sirens send people into planning mode as they discussed what they were going to do to avenge the death. Older people shook their heads in sadness and disappointment because these young people seemed to have little or no regard for human life. They don't realize how precious it is. They don't understand how the loss impacts the families and friends of the victim. They just don't get the fact that it's not TV. You don't get shot, go the emergency room, get fixed up and go home and have a roast beef sandwich. It just doesn't go down like that, except maybe on TV. That's part of the issue - the blurred line between reality and TV and movies. Sometimes when they realize the difference it's too late.

...

As I pulled up to the barbershop, I saw the faces in the crowd and knew that this was probably a fatality. As shots rang out on a summer night and yuppies drank fancy drinks and whispered about summer vacations, a family down the street was about to get the news. Their son had just been shot to death. He was a good kid who was in the wrong place at the wrong time. That young man had hopes, dreams and ambitions that would not be realized this time. His young life snuffed out by bad decisions and intoxicated rivals.

As the crowd gathered and people found out what happened, it turned into a sea of head shaking. People were in disbelief that this could happen in their neighborhood. It seemed as though everyone was left with an overpowering feeling of powerlessness. The exact feeling is hard to describe. As young people arrived on scene, they screamed, some yelled "No! No! No!" and others simply burst into tears. The night dragged on amidst the heat and despair, folks came by with candles to grieve and share at the site of the shooting. Some walked back and forth and some in circles. The atmosphere was filled with disorientation and shock. People hugged, cried and searched for any semblance of relief but it was just not in sight. The night continued and people started to get liquored up and sparked up some weed. It was closing time for my team and I. We could be of no further use that night. Our usual cautions about drug or alcohol use would rest on closed ears. The moon settled into the sky, cabs raced by and another life rose into the night.

...

I was driving from neighborhood to neighborhood checking on local hangouts and just seeing who was posting up when I got a call that someone had been shot. I was informed that it was a point blank shooting. This is unusual because most of the fools who run the streets just pull up and blast whoever's in the area they're pursuing. In this case the shooter hopped out of a car, got into a shooting stance and unloaded four shots into the victim. As family and friends gathered, my staff headed off to the hospital to check on the condition of the victim. The police issued a bulletin for the car involved. While the victim was clinging to life, we were outside the emergency room talking with distraught friends and family. There was speculation about who did it. They each searched for some validation as to why this happened. As raw feelings emerged and emotions flew out of control, police and others worked to restore some semblance of order outside the chaotic ER. It was sure to be another long night for many, including my staff.

In the aftermath of such events we do our best to work with the family and friends of the victim. Sometimes we are sent away because people are disoriented and can't make any decisions or even speak to us. We always leave a card or a number to assist people if they are in need of services beyond the usual. Many staff members have helped families through the burial process providing information and resources about funeral homes, churches, etc. The costs can be very high and very much unexpected so it's all quite challenging. We try to be good listeners and make suggestions if there's an avenue to do so. Many victims have siblings that need a lot of help and someone to share their feelings with in a way and place that they feel comfortable doing so. Believe it or not, sometimes that's a street corner and a playground or just sitting in front of someone's home talking and sharing. It can be a lengthy process as many of our clients have said that people don't know what to say to them. Some folks don't even speak to the victim's families and I believe it's for a variety of reasons. Some think they will say the wrong thing or simply don't know what to say. For others it's just too close to home and is an unfamiliar and uncomfortable place to be.

...

It was another day and another senseless shooting. A young woman clung to life support after having been shot at least three times. Some neighbors said that she was such a good person who really worked hard and wanted to enjoy life. She worked two jobs and had her own apartment. This sounded like a young person who was really going after a good life filled with family and friends. Sadly, she was in the wrong place at the wrong time. As the street speculated on the shooter, anger and rage grew like wildfire. Retaliation seemed imminent as Streetworkers gathered information and tried to find people who can help calm things down and prevent any further violence. It's a tall order indeed! This is the way of the streets. It has no end. It's just the way it is. The sentiment is, "You take out someone from our 'hood and we'll respond with the same." As the week went on, the victim's family was faced with the ultimate decision: whether or not to unplug the life support system that barely maintained their child. This was a challenge beyond words. I will leave this to those who have been there and been faced with it. With little quality of life apparent in her future, she is allowed to go on to perhaps a better place.

My Team and I gathered in the pouring rain outside the Church. The atmosphere was a blend of young people, rain, and tears. I stood in a sea of sadness and wonder. I wondered what she could have done in her life. Many say it would have been good and something special. We simply will never know. As the rain continued, inside the Church she is raised up in a special way, by word and God. She is carried in spirit by those who knew her.

At the burial site, folks continued to grieve and struggle to say goodbye, all oblivious to the pounding rain. Streetworkers spread throughout the crowd and shared and listened to young people who wanted to talk. One Streetworker stayed with the father of the deceased and held an umbrella over him as he stared into the grave, lost in shock, disbelief, and love. As others went to their cars, the father and the Streetworker stayed and stared. Eventually the worker walked the father to the family car. He later told me that he felt the need to stay with the father because he is a father himself. It was all very close to home. The thought of losing a child is a potential nightmare for the Streetworker. He knows that violence has no parameters, no guidelines, and no ethics. There is no one who is off limits or untouchable. Violence can strike anywhere at any time. It makes for a steady concern for parents of young people who live in the City. Many times young people complain about parents who are always on them to share their location, whether it is via text or phone call. The above incident is one reason why. Parents feel that their children are always in harm's way and have to be very much aware of their surroundings.

...

As I moved on to the next challenge, I struggled to take an emotional breather. I was dealing with two murders in one week. A young eighteen year old man crossed into the wrong place at the wrong time. For him, it was just a stop at a convenience store, but to others it was an infringement on their space. Consequently, they felt the need to kill this guy. By all accounts, he wasn't even involved in any gang activity. There are no rules or guidelines governing the streets. They knew where he lived and decided to stab him to death. He was a young man known to many, mostly through playing baseball in various leagues around Boston. He was known for always laughing and clowning around, not known to hurt or bother anyone.

As Streetworkers congregated at the funeral home, the victim's family and extended family gathered together for prayer. Rest assured there is no rest. No rest for those who had to endure this unexpected and inescapable pain. Pain dealt at the hand of someone who had little, if any, value for life. As I looked around at that sad scene I wondered about the perpetrator? Was he having dinner somewhere? Was he out at the movies? Did he realize the impact and finality of what he'd done? Did he have a conscience and if so, did it bother him at all? If he saw this room full of people crying would it impact him? There were so many questions!

There were some people from a rival territory who come to pay respect to the victim. This was a bold move. The word was that they were blood relatives of the deceased. Nevertheless their presence made for some dramatic tension.

Streetworkers and others outside and in the funeral home tried to get accurate word around that these people were in fact distant family members. The volatility of this event had to be addressed at a street level, as best as it could be. I hoped that no one from the victim's family would seek vengeance upon these guests. The worry was that raw feelings would overtake any reasoning. The night went on and the situation remained tense but tolerable.

As services came to an end, the mother of the victim raged against the closing of the casket. Her son would be cremated and so that was it. Someone brought her a chair so she could sit in front of the casket alone and have her time alone with her son. People slowly backed away. After a few minutes, her spirit exploded with a sea of tears and grief. Many tried to comfort her but it was just not going to happen. Many people lingered outside of the Church. They were holding buttons with the deceased's picture on it. Some held tight to the beautiful program that was filled the happier and wonderful moments of his short life. As the night grew darker the cold air nudged the crowd and sent them along looking for warmer places. They dispersed gradually, each carrying some memories of another friend gone too soon. RIP

...

The yellow crime scene tape blew about the street, while neighbors whispered and shared faces of concern and fear. It was another killing that the spirit finds hard to make sense of. Yuppies passed by with little interest as to what had happened. There was a sense that some knew but did not want to inquire as to what took place. A sort of denial encompasses parts of the community at times. There's a "not in my neighborhood" type of attitude about things.

The victim's close friends are filled with anger and rage. They talked amongst themselves about revenge and potential aggressors who might have killed their friend. They posed questions to one another: Had he posted a video on the Internet? Did he have a beef in school? Maybe it's over a relationship? The conversation encompassed the crowd in search of someone to hold accountable for the taking of a friends' life.

As anger grew and some people turned to alcohol and pot, the police kept a close but distant eye on the group. There is an unwritten protocol for things like this. People are given space as long as they keep it contained and do not impact passersby or disrupt the neighborhood. As the night turned to cold, the crowd waned, taking home their grief and sorrow marinated in a sense of uncertainty.

It's very difficult to even attempt to reason with people, especially young people, when they are totally overwhelmed with the death of a friend. I can try my best to pick a spot for a delicate conversation, but the opportunity can fade very quickly. The bottom line is I have to try. There are times when, among a flurry of expletives, I may get a word in that can make a difference. Sometimes I simply never know or never find out. It's like when you have heard the same advice over and over and then, one day, it sinks in. That's the hope and prayer that I can impact a young person even though they don't look like they are hearing me.

The world of gang life is very difficult to describe,

traverse, and understand. I am reminded of an old adage, "Seek not to know the answers, only to understand the questions." Young people are influenced by so many things not the least of which is the media. Electronic media is so prevalent and in my view, does not offer a lot of positive things for young people. Granted we can chose what we which to view but the market flooding of negative behavior and venues can be daunting, especially to a young person. As young people strive to find their path and fit in, there can be a lot of confusion and misunderstanding.

We all need to fit in somewhere. Let's start with family. What is a person's sense of family? What if there is no Dad and no positive role models in a kid's path? Where do they look for guidance and direction? There was a time when a kid would look mostly to a teacher, Priest, coach or close relative. I just don't see it being as common anymore. The design and structure of a family is so different. There is no more *set* dinner time. There is no more being home when the street lights come on. These were simple yet fundamental signs of structure in a family at one time. I grew up in a single parent home with my Mom. She used what she could to develop some guidelines towards establishing some kind of normalcy and foundation as to how we would function and move as a unit. No, it wasn't perfect but if you weren't home at supper time, you may not eat until the next day. That was a fact in my world and I'm sure many of my peers. These days kids come and go as they please grabbing a sandwich or something to eat here and there.

Church was also another place to find a sense of structure

and consistency. Many Sundays I didn't want to get up for services but I did. My mother would make sure I did. I think somehow she knew that this is and would continue to be important in life. It's crucial to give young people a place to feel safe and find some security, a place of hope and love. In prayer, I instinctively know that I am heard. That's the only way I can explain it. Most of my neighbors and friends went to Church and experienced the Sacraments.

Churches, Temples or Synagogues are all places to be considered as a constant place to grow along spiritual lines and find some hope and peace. In sharing with clergy folks and others in the black community, I suggested creating some services specifically for youth. As a Catholic, my youth group was always an hour to an hour and a half. There was always the option to stay longer or to come back to Church at any time. In my opinion, a young person will not sit in a service for three or so hours. Instead, I suggest short youth focused services to give young people a taste of their religion and let them decide if they want to pursue things a bit more. They should also be allowed to participate if it's at all possible. Frankly, I would have never survived a two or three hour service, which is most common in some Churches. This would be an instant resentment for me and would have found me looking for guidance elsewhere as I got older. Many young people today do not have a true connection to their faith. Some go through the motions to satisfy their parents. There needs to be a real conversation about how to present faith to kids. We have to do a much better job of sharing and also listening to their understanding of things. The need has never been stronger and the challenge has never been greater. Listen…

…

Over the course of a week a lot of shots fired were fired in the same neighborhood, seemingly at the same group of people. That is one corner I don't recommend chillin' on anytime soon! As Streetworkers pursued their usual avenues of information, the consensus was that something pretty big had happened to bring on such a massive barrage of gunfire in one small area. As word came in from various sources it seemed that someone bought some dope using counterfeit money. This was really not a good idea. We all know "they" can't call the cops but when you take my money, and it's a lot of money, you can call someone. I had to wonder what these clowns were thinking. Did they really think they could get away with this? So, the shootings were for those who took the money and the dope. I realized that probably no one involved here went to business school, but they should know that it just doesn't work that way. At that point the thieves were trying to find the right people to make contact and make it right. A Streetworker was trying to get the message to the shooters about it but they were not feeling in a mood to receive messages about compensation and fixing the "mistake." They needed to get a message out: that a high price will be paid for trying something like that. No honor among thieves for sure. This was going to be a tough one to negotiate and work to prevent further violence on any level. If you can't influence directly you need to find someone who can. I needed someone who could ask folks to back off for just a bit, to cool down, and then go forward with what needs to happen to make it right, if anything. This could easily cost someone their life. It could also cost an innocent bystander their life. Someone simply waiting at the bus stop in this area could be targeted. When folks want revenge they will take it out on anyone who is in their path. I have seen this way too many times.

. . .

It was just at sundown in the summer when shots were heard near a local park. A crowd descended upon the crime scene amidst a squad of police cars from all directions, people jockeyed for position to see who the victim was. No one could tell who the victim was as the yellow crime scene police tape was being spread and officers told people to back up away from the scene. A blue blanket covered the body (which was an apparent homicide). He must have been hit with a lot of shots because he was covered fairly quickly compared to other scenes I've been to. A young man came up screaming and yelling about the identity of the victim. He kept asking those around him if they'd seen his brother. Some said no and others shook their heads left to right. He was frantic as he continued to work his way through the crowd with a look of overt desperation. He finally ran into a close friend who said, "Call your brothers cell phone. He might be around here somewhere." As the call went through, there was a ringing from under the blanket where the victim lay. It was like slow motion as this young man realized his brother was the shooting victim. He had to be restrained by police and friends as he made a vain attempt to get to his brothers body. There was no more mystery, just sadness. Tears spread over the crowd in pseudo disbelief. People knew this happens but its home now as it happened here. The crowd wrestled with its' feelings and slowly dissipated into the gathering darkness.

...

It was a nice sunny day people went about their business, mothers passed by with baby carriages, seniors enjoyed their day in the park watching the children and neighbors played with their dogs. My local Streetworker called and said one of his kids was shot late last night. He told me that the victim's friends were on the hunt for the shooter (who most likely lives in an adjacent neighborhood). He told me he needed to find them before they did something stupid and that they were on bicycles. So, I picked him up and we started to ride through the 'hood where his boys were looking. It was a beautiful afternoon and local people had little or no idea what was going on. It seemed so contradictory to such a day that violence was at the forefront of this community, at least for the moment. We rode along with hope and concern that we may find these guys before they act. We knew they are driven by anger. Their feelings and guns were cocked with an emotional hairpin trigger that could be set off very quickly. We were on a desperate journey. We circled the housing project with wide eyes and anxiety. Time was of the essence for sure. No one is spotted as we continued our search for a bit and then headed back towards the other 'hood.

As we made a corner, the Streetworker spotted one of the young guys on his bike. His face told me he was intent on one thing and was not doing something good. I can't just roll up on him. He doesn't know my car and we could get shot that way. I went down the street and let my Streetworker out so he could make his way back and find this guy. He clearly was a shooter so we need to get to him.

I rode around hoping to hear back from staff as to what happened with this guy. I was hopeful that we were able to talk with him and calm him down a bit. Maybe get him to wait a day. We needed to do whatever would work to at least delay any action that will impact a bunch of families.

The purpose of trying to delay violence is the hope that with a little extra time people will come to their sense and find some reason to step back from their intentions. It can be quite a process to convince a young person to take a different course. I have to hope and pray that it will happen. A Streetworker may remind a guy about his son, daughter, little brother or perhaps his mom. Does he want to leave them to fend for themselves if he gets hit or is in jail? It's a potential reality and attempts to get someone to think things all the way through, have been a lifesaver at times. As I said, it's process and a delicate one at that. Streetworkers have to be very careful how you approach someone who is angry and intent on revenge. My workers have to weigh their relationship and then determine the best approach.

There are times when the help of a family member or in-law is needed to impact the thinking of a person who is intent on responding to a violent act perpetrated against a friend or fellow gang member. There is a quiet desperation in a Streetworkers heart as he knows about the possibilities and will utilize any resources he can find to stop potential violence. It's a challenge to the soul and spirit for sure. I have often reminded staff that we are not responsible for a person's actions or lack thereof. WE can help people search out their options and hope they make healthy decisions.

…

As I attempted to enjoy my morning coffee, a text came in that someone had been shot late that night. Yes, it knocked me off my beam a bit. I always look forward to the morning because it's the most peaceful time of the day. That was not the case on that particular morning! So, I started to work the phone to gather more information as to the origin and nature of the violence. What *set* is it, if any? Does anyone on staff know the victim or his family? We have to explore our circle of influence to see if we can impact the situation via support or the diversion or future violence. Sometimes I am simply told to step off and back out because there's too much trauma and history between the parties involved. It may simply be in the hands of law enforcement to deal with it.

On the heels of this need I learned that there was also a young woman who was been shot at the same location. As people tried to find out what happened, a Streetworker went to the hospital to offer support to the shooting victim's family. Upon approaching the emergency room, there was a small contingent of very upset people, relatives and friends. They paced with anxiety amidst a cloud of smoke and wonder. The fact was someone knew who did this and the challenge was to impact the situation in hopes of getting people to understand hat this should be dealt with in the right way. The question is: ﹒t was the right way? The legal system? Street justice? If ﹒ew who did it you can be assured that they know you ﹒o retaliate and be ready for you. Do we need more people hurt or killed? What about street credibility? Respect? Honor? If there is no response does it mean you can come by anytime and shoot anyone you want and there will be no price to pay? These are tough questions with real life answers.

How do you decide when you're lost in a sea of anger, rage, and sadness? Sometimes folks will verbalize what violence they are going to exact upon someone and say they don't care what happens after that. A Streetworker can help a person postpone their response via spending time with the victim's family and friends. I can hope and pray that they will come to their senses. I can't imagine the process that takes place during this time. I imagine the questions that the human spirit is confronted with. There is often a denial of the victim's part in his or her situation. It's no time for pointing fingers but people eventually have to be honest with themselves. If you shoot at someone they may shoot back - maybe not the same day, but someday. They also may see or find a friend or relative who they deem an easier target. There are no rules, no ethics and no guidelines in the world of violence. People decide as they go along.

...

Silence captured one early evening but not for long. Dudes lurked in the basements and backrooms of the 'hood getting smoked up and tapping on some Hennessey for a quick high. It's a simple recipe for disaster when people carrying guns get high. Nothing good will ever come from that combination. Down the street, people scurried from the transit station as they made their way towards home. Then the sound of the gunfire rang out and people recognize the "pop" that they are familiar with. Faces of fear and concern continued on their way as wonder spreads over the crowd. It's not like you can run down the street and see what's going on. If there's a fire, folks will go down and see what's going on, but not gunfire.

Several guys had been shot while sitting in a car. There was an ethnic festival going on and there was speculation it may have had something to do with the aftermath of that. Maybe some people got too high or maybe there were two groups beefing that met up. The police said it was retaliation for a crime committed last year. That doesn't really help people in the field of street work because we needed to narrow it down.

Timing is so crucial in street work. The sharing of information is crucial to preventing further violence. One cannot prevent further violence without knowing the reason behind the incident. There's almost always one. At that point, we can assess the options to deter what may happen in the future. A common strategy is to ask people to delay their intentions. This may be regarding retaliation or just plain beef with another set. This is one of the best strategies sometimes. There is a chance that people will come to their senses when they wait a day or two before reacting in a violent manner. You have to take my word for it. It happens. It is hard to document when things have been prevented.

· · ·

One afternoon, I heard that a multiple shooting has ┤ the life of one of our young people. This was a kid been in and out of the office, so many staff members knew him. That hard-to-accept feeling started to take over. We were reminded that is not a job but a mission, a mission to help extended family. The relationships are real and healthy and positive. They are relationships of struggle and challenge and setback. When one human being puts a lot of time in with another human being, the bond is set. No, it's not perfect, but it's there, with all its imperfections and pushback's.

The news about the death of this young man spread quickly to all staff. Support is brought forth and shared. We are the people who know the pain and peers are the best support. I believe in my line of work you can't go home and share this stuff with your spouse or family really. It's too much violence and death. It would be a serious stressor to any relationship. So, we sit in our conference room sharing a lot but saying nothing. We are afraid of our raw feelings and the sharing of such in a public setting. We will pick those in the room whom we trust the most and take it outside of the office to share. It's a lonely place to be. We share but we don't speak. We feel but we stuff and hide our feelings in a place that's secret and untouchable, so we think. Many of us are street kids so there's a genuine toughness nurtured by experiences in the 'hood. The feelings aren't foreign but they are still very uncomfortable. We are restless and withdrawn, a hard shell waiting to be cracked. People get up from the conference table and head out to the neighborhood. They are strapped with little hope today. As the afternoon darkened, the Streetworker tried to think of ways to somehow, someway, rise to meet the immediate needs of young people who would demand answers about the death of their friend.

...

Snow whipped around the crowd gathered outside the Church. Inside, sadness and anger swirled uncontrolled as a young man was memorialized and attempts were made to lay him to rest. He had been doing well. I know this is said all the time, but he really was heading in a different direction. He had done some time in jail and had seemed to learn his lesson there. Once again, the streets don't forget what you've done. Others around you may take joy in your new path, but those who run the streets don't forgive and forget. So, when you're on your way home from work or a local basketball game and someone recognizes you, it may be time to collect a debt for pain and violence experienced by someone awhile back. That's the case here. When someone gets shot in broad daylight in a crowded bus station, it's obvious that it's personal.

This funeral brought people out that haven't been seen in a long time. The deceased was is the younger brother of someone who used to play the game years ago. The thought of retired gangsters picking up weapons again is a real problem. You don't want to get these older guys started, but when someone takes out someone you love, the shooter will be held accountable. As Streetworkers played through the crowd, it just didn't seem possible to sell the thought of asking folks to keep their wits and head about them. There was too much anger and rage to even initiate such a discussion. I could only say a few words of comfort and say a silent prayer that they make it into the hearts of anyone who will listen. There was a prevalent sense that revenge would be taken and done so in a swift manner. There were a large number of shooters there and some were high and strapped. They were ready and willing to use their weapons.

It's a delicate balance at the funeral as police in marked and unmarked cars skirted the perimeter. They posted up at either end of the street to dissuade or stop any potential intruders from riding by. They maintained their positions out of respect and public safety for all. It was a delicate process at a venue like this. The night before this funeral there was a vigil held in the community in remembrance of the victim. As a crowd gathered around the site, candlelight tempered the emotions of some and lit the same in others. Out of nowhere, a young man emerged and started taunting the crowd and that they had "bodied" one of y'all and flashing his gang's sign. This caught everyone by surprise, even the police who were sitting in their cruiser. They could see there was some commotion and started exiting the car. This guy came and went in one of those slow motion type moments where you're not sure this just happened. How could he have the balls or is it insanity, to step up on a group like this and proclaim some type of ownership for the deceased. This was totally off the hook. My feeling is he would have been shot many times if the police were not there. Who knows how many innocent people could have been shot as well.

It's no secret that people in the crowd at the vigil had weapons on them. It's just the way it is. This incident really left me speechless. I still can't believe that an enemy set had someone come by the vigil site and threaten people like that. It just says that there are no boundaries, rules or ethics about any of this stuff. What kind of person would do this? It makes you wonder if some people need medication? A person would need to have no concern for their own life or the life of others to do this. It is virtual suicide to make such an outrageous statement and act up in such a solemn venue as a vigil. I believe the police saved a lot of people from being shot just by their presence.

…

It is an exceptional challenge to the spirit when a young person you have previously sat with face to face, is shot and killed. There is something even more personal than the obvious tragedy of a young person's violent death. I often wonder if there was something I could have said, and didn't, that may have made the difference. It spawns an eternal guessing game that will lead nowhere but a path that will be traveled. It's simply human nature to wonder if I could have made a difference that would have brought different results.

None of us can really claim the victory or defeat of another human being. Human nature affords us free will and sometimes we are the victims of our own best thinking. This young guy was only eighteen years old. He was driving around on a Saturday night and probably doing what some young people do on Saturday nights. He may have been temporarily worry-free. Apparently someone recognized him and felt a need to settle a score. About ten shots were fired toward the vehicle. That was it. It was probably all very surreal when it was happening. One minute he was chilllin' and the next he had a problem.

There was a strong stench of violence with blood on the windows and seats. The driver made an attempt to make it to the hospital but fell a couple of miles short. The police were in pursuit and the car slowly pulled over. The passenger was pronounced dead on the scene. That night and his life were over and things would never be the same. Both of their families will be impacted forever.

My team and I made our way to the emergency room at hospital. It was an emotional wave of sadness that took us through the door. The emergency room was a very unique place because each person was there with an immediate need and the staff needed to rise to the challenge with incredible sensitivity, restraint, and emotional awareness. They really had to be on top of things and fully aware at all times. When a victim of violence comes through the door, so does their family and friends who usually so with a vengeance, and eventually, with a mission to find out who put their loved one in this place. In this instance, the Hospital Staff couldn't share any information with a mom who demanded to see her son. The nurse struggled to bring the mom to some sense of gathering herself but it's not going to happen. The mom received word her son has been shot and would not stop without an immediate answer.

Family and friends started getting out of control and throwing things and tipping over stuff. Security Staff tried their best to contain people without arresting anyone. It was a difficult task to walk the fine line between understanding and maintaining the integrity and security of the ER. After much commotion, a staff member informed the mother that her son was not there. The nurse was fighting back tears when she revealed this information because she was not supposed to divulge anything. Her heart was heavy because she had no further information except the fact that the victim is not there. The fact is that he was still at the crime scene...in the car... where he had been pronounced dead.

The Police had to do their job by gathering evidence and that had left a huge space in the process for the family. The overwhelming sense of loss, powerlessness, and the tragic feeling of not being able to help in any way had taken over. The victim's mother really lost it now and family members do their best to comfort her. My sense was that people would hold on to hope until they actually saw the body. This seemed logical to me. After all, there were two guys shot so maybe the other guy, not her son, had passed. Believe it or not, this had happened before - where the person thought killed was actually alive and the alleged survivor was actually gone. It's not common but it can happen as information gets passed along.

So, it was a long night in the ER. The place got crowded as it filled with those in need of services. Family and friends gathered outside in a cloud of sadness and anger, as cigarette smoke and hope rose into the night. R.I.P.

Prior to his passing I met with the victim. At the time he was incarcerated. Sometimes it's good to have a captive audience. He had spoken about his dreams of his own "crib", "whip" and finding a good woman. I never want to push back on a person's dreams. There is a delicate conversation somewhere between reality and fantasy. I try to get a person to think about the steps toward a dream and also the steps that will end it quickly. At times, the ego gets in the way. There is a sense of entitlement that dreams will come to fruition. "Don't you know who I am?" Sadly, you have to pursue things like the rest of the world does. You have to move forward with steps in place. He had people to support him. You pay a price for alleged shortcuts toward pursuing material things especially.

After his death my staff and I sat in the office amid tears of a broken and ended life. It was just very sad and very frustrating to think that another young person was gone and gone way too young. What else could we have said to him?

…

The path of violence continues to pave its' way through the community. As two young men were shot near a local pharmacy, details emerged that made things even more disturbing. It appeared that two young men were ordered to attack a rival group who were hanging out on a corner down the block a bit. It was no secret that they were terrified but were about to do what they were told by higher ranking members of their set. As they set upon their prey, their nerves and intestinal fortitude were pushed to the max. They decided to shoot at their targets from across the street. They did so and each of them emptied their clips without hitting anyone. Well, this is a mistake in any venue. They were quickly set upon and paid the ultimate price. This was all in broad daylight.

One of the things that comes to mind here is the desperation of the shooters, who went there to "put some work in." The level of fear and terror of this situation is beyond measure. When a young person gets to that point, there's no turning back. The fear factor in pursuit of attempting to kill someone is off the hook. What happens to the human spirit when you're clip is empty and you are now the target? It's really over the top. The thought of what someone experiences when they are in this type of situation is incomprehensible. I'm sure it wasn't even considered when they set upon this mission. They went on their quest with the intent that someone would be killed and someone was. So, the night settled in as crime scene tape blew down the street and folks had access to pick up their supplies at the pharmacy again. The night moved on.

...

Sometimes a Streetworker, like other human service workers, sits home at night and wonders about some of the people they are trying to help. It can be a futile effort at times but the thing is this: you never know when someone will get it. You don't know when someone will get the idea that the gang life is a dead end. There is no glory in an early grave or jail. The frustration to get that message through requires a resilient spirit with constant vigilance and determination. You don't want to give up before the miracle happens and you just don't know when that will be. Sometimes a Streetworker will get a call in the middle of the night. It may be about a shooting or it may be about some drama about to go down.

A recent late night caller told the Streetworker there was a shooting and one person was hit. As the cops showed up and the victim was taken to hospital the police scoured the area for weapons, evidence, etc. They didn't find what one of the victims friends' found. One of the shooters had lost his cell phone out of pocket and these guys found it. Turn it into the police? Hell no! They're not going to do that. They called a few numbers in it to see who would answer and thus get a better idea of where the shooter was from and who he posts with. It was all clear now and the path to revenge was laid out...in a contact list on a cell phone. The word spread about where the gunners were from and talk kicked in about when to ride on those dudes. It was known where they chilled. I wondered if they had any idea that they were about to be set upon in the most violent way. Had the shooter realized his phone was missing in all the excitement? Did he think he lost it at home or maybe during his flight from the crime scene? Timing can be everything. It could save a life. It is certain that once the word got out about this, no one would be hanging on that corner for a while. It just wouldn't be smart, but then again, these guys don't care too much about this stuff. They'll be out there carrying *something* with them for protection or whatever. There's simply no good end in sight. Cars and dreams pass slowly in the night. You can only wonder ...

Jake Manning

Chapter 14: Solutions

The term "holistic approach" is the description that comes to mind and is definitely the only way to find some progress and solution toward the issues of violence in any community. People think the police can do it and that others as well can do it. It's clear that everyone has a part to play here. I realize this is not a profound observation so let's get to it.

Let's start with responsibility and environment. The government is not responsible to raise our children. The schools and other institutions will have an impact but they are not the sole force behind the raising of a child. Children start their day hopefully with some sort of breakfast and head off to school. They get out of school in the afternoon, may stop at home for a minute, then they're out the door. With a little luck, they may come back home for some dinner - if there is any. Then they go back outside and return home at hopefully by 9pm (depending on their age and circumstances). Considering all of this time out of the house it is important to ask, "Where does a kid actually grow up?"

It seems to me that they grow up in the streets with the rest of the kids. If this is the case, where do they learn values? Who tells them what is right or wrong? How do these kids learn what type of behavior is acceptable? Who sets the standard for a young person to establish human and social values? When it comes to answering these questions there is quite a bit to think and get honest about.

The responsibility to raise a child starts at home. Being a parent is the most challenging job with the least qualifications in the entire world. I don't think any parent would dispute this. The dialogue has to be started and maintained between a parent and a child. I know many parents who say they are a parent to their child and not necessarily a friend. There are some semantics involved in defining this.

In the world I've seen, you cannot smoke a joint with your teenage child and then demand that the child get up to go to school. It's just not going to work. I have met some single parents in very lonely situations. These parents need a friend and actually go to one of their own kids to socialize. Before you know it, this parent is seen by the child's friends as a peer and they are all getting high together. To them it's all good but in reality it is desperation with a high priced impact on a struggling family. There is no good ending in a situation like this. Dysfunction begins at home and is then carried out into the world.

It's a tough thing to negotiate with a young person coming from this type of environment. You can't really criticize someone's parent or the wall goes up and it's over. How do we impact and influence a young person's values without criticizing what they already believe to be ok because they learned it at home? These kids don't know that they don't know.

I believe the Church or any religious institution is a huge part of the solution here. I grew up poor in the housing project but I still had Church. My mother made sure I got up and off to services. No, I didn't want to go but looking back, it made a lifesaving difference as I went along in the real world. I always knew God was there and at least I had a Higher Power to ask for help-which I definitely needed when I got in many jams as

I got older. There's a huge part of hope that lies in the walls of a Church, Temple, Synagogue or Mosque. There has to be somewhere or something to go to when there is nothing else human available.

Over the years I have met some young people who admitted that they prayed for help when they were jammed up. So, I believe it is something these young kids want and will accept if encouraged. Attending religious services is good on many levels. The chance of meeting other good folks at a religious institution is likely. People are there for the same reason so it's inevitable that a young person will meet other good kids to chill with and do so in a constructive manner. No one expects perfection but it's possible to find ethics and morals that can become part of a young person's fiber.

I used to run a Church Youth Group on Friday nights. The group grew to about 50-70 young people. It was a simple format entitled *Pizza and Prayer* and that's what it was! We would say a few simple prayers and folks could talk; we would sing a song or two, eat pizza and share a healthy dose of social activity (i.e. video and board games, etc.). It was safe and fun and that is why it was successful. Parents were thrilled to know their kids were in a safe place on a Friday night. I ran a tight ship and no one was allowed in after a certain time and no one could leave until it was time to do so. Parents would call occasionally to make sure their child was in attendance. It was all good and I really enjoyed being part of such a positive program, especially on a Friday night.

I encourage parents to enroll their children in any structured program especially one that operates on Fridays and Saturdays. These two days are some of the key times when people get into trouble - sometimes because they're bored, and sometimes because they are simply making bad decisions. There are many choices to make. Young people have great options at Community Centers, Boys and Girls Clubs, YMCA, YWCA and other social outlets. If a kid gets involved young enough he may stay involved and once again, meet some good young people who are doing the right thing and having fun. There are also many adults available in these venues to go to if a young person has an issue or problem that they want to share or need advice about. Most staff members are trained to tell young people about their availability to help and encourage them to come forward if they need anything.

I remember always telling young people, "I'm not necessarily smarter than you, I've just lived longer." When someone came to me, I would be careful to share my experience and not be judgmental, unless I was specifically asked my opinion on any given situation.

I also found success in turning a negative into a positive by depersonalizing a situation and then presenting it. For example, I was informed when I worked at a school of a bullying situation led by two girls. I decided to form an anti-bullying committee to work on a program to address bullying. I asked the two main bullies to be part of the five person committee. They had no idea I knew about their actions. In the process of this committee involvement, they became empowered and turned their intentions around. The committee was praised and held in esteem. There was no finger pointing and accusations. This was all started because the young girl who was being bullied had the courage to come forward and tell me in the strictest confidence what was going on. It was not snitching, she did the right thing! As for the two bullies, they wanted power and ultimately they got it but in a positive way.

An early start to develop some structure for young people can make all the difference. Let's encourage young people to take advantage of programs in schools, churches, and all the other places where good things are available. There's simply not a lot of good going on out at the street corner. I believe we need to dig deeper in the process of instilling respect in our young people as well. It's the one thing people will say is missing today as compared to yesterday. It starts with self-respect in terms of taking care of oneself physically, mentally and spiritually. Some young kids need to be taught about hygiene and taking care of their physical being. I've been amazed how lacking this has been over the years. A kid has to be taught to take care of his body by showering, brushing teeth, wearing clean clothing and presenting himself in a decent manner.

Personal responsibility needs to be at the forefront. Respect and personal responsibility are really not that prominent in the lives of young people. They are certainly not where they need to be. There needs to be a lot of discussions about all the issues that impact the world of a young person. We could use schools or other places where a captive audience can take place.

There are many options for groups to meet in any given community. My experience has taught me that young people love to talk about the issues. It helps them sort it all out and establish their own values and do so in a constructive way. I can't tell you how many times I've heard the statement, "I didn't know that." If no one tells our young people they are at the mercy of the media which is not a good thing.

Let's help to mold our young people so they know the difference between friendship and dating and what each means and entails. Let's talk about drugs and alcohol and what harm they can do, especially at a young age. Drugs will absolutely impact decision making and a person's future. How many kids do we know who did something under the influence that they would have never done sober?

It's vital for the recovery community to step up and be more proactive, especially in communities of color. There are many free resources to combat drug and alcohol abuse and people need to avail themselves of such. Many 12-step programs have easy access and should be taken advantage of where needed and wanted. At this point, they are simply underutilized. Everyone knows there is a direct connection between violence and substance abuse, so let's help folks get to the root of the problem.

Society is desperate for good people to step forward as well. We have so many good programs and opportunities but we need mentors. I believe an hour or two a week to help a young person is a small sacrifice where the rewards can be much greater than one would think. I have had some great human experiences just sitting and talking with a young person. Many are grateful that someone cares enough to listen. There is nothing more valuable to give someone than love and time.

Let's talk about courage and doing the right thing. Yes, it takes courage to step up when you see something wrong or about to go wrong. We know there is always something you can do, without compromising your safety. Let's encourage young people in this direction. They need encouragement and support to head in this direction.

We need more trips to college campuses to help young people get excited about education. I remember a time I took some young folks to Boston College for a women's basketball game. As we were getting out of the van, a young woman said, "Why are we coming here? We'll never go to school here." I said, "Do you want to go here? If you want to go here and work toward that goal, there are people who will help you to get into school here." She had initiated the conversation that I wanted to hear. Those are the discussions I want to take place. That is what the main purpose of the trip was. Let's get young people on campus so they can look around and maybe spark some questions and discussion. Most trips will bring about this conversation regarding college or other avenues to pursue.

Some young people have it imbedded in them that they are going nowhere. Some feel that they may not live very long. There seems to be an intrinsic cynicism when it comes to the future. We have to challenge and overcome that type of thinking. We have to reach inside and find a young person's passion for life

I believe each of us has an innate desire to find our place in the world and we cannot allow fear or lack of confidence to shut us down. Today's youth have to understand that there will be pushback, hardship, lots of setbacks and temptation to veer off the path. They have to learn to think things all the way through. If it feels right inside and there is that gut feeling that it is a good thing, then go for it. Our instincts answer most of our questions.

My hope is that young people realize or come to realize that there are many people who believe in them. There are people who care everywhere; they just have to be sought out. Young people should search out positive role models in school, Church, sports coaches, family friends and family. They need to stay focused, stay strong, and step up for themselves. With the trust and love of a gracious God or Higher Power, a hopeful community, and a passion to make a difference for themselves and others, success will follow. Are you a victim or a survivor?

It is imperative for young people to step back in to the world and regain their own power. Nurture, energize, and strengthen the human spirit! The sky's the limit when you create your positive energy. Today is the day to start doing things better on behalf of you!

One Nation Inside the Bricks

Jake Manning

Glossary of Terms

1. set: gang
2. whip: car
3. work, putting some work in: shooting at some one
4. bricks, projects: housing project
5. burner, heater, toast, : gun
6. ride, ride on: go to another sets territory with intent
7. crib: home, house
8. joint: jail/prison
9. dirt: violence
10. projects, bricks: public housing development

To Joanna.
With Love, Hope
+
Peace.

John

31832614R00081

Made in the USA
Charleston, SC
30 July 2014